The Roche Family

NELSON'S
FAMILY CAMPGROUND

*A collection of memories from
Nelson's Campground*

By Nelson Gustine

50 Years - 2014

Nelson Gustine

Prentis Printing Solutions, Inc.
Meriden, Connecticut

Nelson's Family Campground
71 Mott Hill Rd.
East Hampton, CT 06424
860-267-5300 FAX 860-267-8956
Email: Nelsonsfamilycampground@msn.com
Website: Nelsoncampground.com

Cover image created by Ford Folios, Inc.
Back cover photo used with permission from
National Association of RV Parks and Campgrounds (ARVC)

ISBN: 978-0-9892046-2-0

Printed in the United States of America

In loving memory
of Mildred Gustine

This book was written in memory of my wife,
Mildred, to whom I was married 53 years. Mil and
I hit it off together in the very beginning. I could not
have built the campground without her. We had a
marriage that was made in heaven. We never said
a cross word in anger. Losing her in 2009 was the
saddest thing that ever happened in my life.
I love her very much.

Acknowledgements

I would like to say thank you to many people for all the help they gave me in the beginning when cash was scarce and work was plentiful. Number one is my father-in-law, Fred Kaiser. He was at my side building the campground but, unfortunately, didn't live long enough to see the Rec. hall completed. We named the Rec. hall "Kaiser Hall" after him.

Al Turner helped me build the campground and loved to drive my bulldozer, especially when building the pond. Al Brilliant got Area G under control. Shawn Webster, Gordon Campbell and Tammy Strong helped in the beginning and still work at the campground.

Paul Dunphy and Butch Kuhn helped keep the Civil War program going. Dolores Dunphy, Karen Kuhn, Dolly Lawrence, Carlene Schultz, Cora Pierce, and Lil Turner helped start the store and initiated some of the craft and activity programs. The Botsacos family helped with many chores at the campground.

I would like to thank Roberta J. Buland for her assistance in getting my book started and creating the chapters. Thanks also to Cora Sciarra and Peggy Lezon for their help editing, proofreading, typesetting, and formatting over 100 pictures to fit in this book.

Without the help of my two sons, Bruce and Glenn, it would have been difficult to realize my dream. I especially want to thank Michele Gustine for doing such a great job running the campground.

Because so many people helped with the book over a period of time, in a variety of ways, I would like to extend my heartfelt thanks and appreciation.

TABLE OF CONTENTS

1

The Growth of Nelson

I always looked at myself as being adventurous. When I was fourteen years old, I dreamed of joining the Navy and going to China. I don't know why, but I always had that in my head.

In August, 1938, I decided that I wanted to go camping. I tried to get some of my buddies to go with me. Finally, I found a friend from school who said he'd go. My mother knew about a campground in East Hampton, Connecticut, called Hart's Village. We could put up a tent there, so off we went. We camped for the whole month by ourselves and had a great time.

The tent was about six feet high and twelve feet wide. It didn't come waterproofed, so we waterproofed it — or thought we did. We painted gasoline on it with paraffin. Later on, the combination of paraffin and gasoline caused the Hartford Circus Fire, but that's another story.

I don't remember if we had cots in the tent or slept on blankets. As a teenager, it didn't really matter. We had blankets for covers, though, because we knew it got cold at night. We had a little stove to cook outdoors. It wasn't like a Coleman stove. It used charcoal. We put the charcoal in a basin and strips of metal to grill hamburgers on top of it. But, we hardly used it because every time we wanted to, it rained! In fact, it rained almost the entire month!

One day, two Italian girls who were camping nearby felt so sorry for us that they sent over a great big bowl of potato salad. It had onions in it, and neither my friend nor I liked onions. I can still picture us sitting there picking out the onions!

At the end of August, my parents came to visit us. They camped with me because they thought camping was a good thing to do. My sister was excited about it, too. So we continued camping on weekends in September. That year, the Great Hurricane came to Connecticut. As it went through the camp, it left a lot of wreckage. It knocked our tent over to one side, but other places were totally demolished.

The next year, 1939, I still had a desire to do something different. I was in high school where the Citizens' Military Training Camp (CMTC) was offered as part of the U.S. Army at Fort Devens, Massachusetts. Three or four other fellows and I signed up. We learned army maneuvers in August. Everybody said we were crazy because Hitler was on the move, and we would be the first ones to go and fight. We said, "No, we're gonna train you guys to go." It became a comedy.

Hazel Gustine camping at Hart's Village

In 1940, we pitched our tent at the same campsite, and my family and I went there weekends. A portable cottage was for sale there. My father bought it and we continued camping there.

After graduating from high school I worked with my father. The Second World War was going full speed then. I still dreamed of joining the Navy. Business was slow for my Dad. So in 1943, I went to Coyne Electrical School, in Chicago. Then I joined the Navy to fulfill my dream. I was twenty years old, just a kid, really.

I went to New Haven, Connecticut, to enlist. I was sent to boot camp in Rhode Island, and then got a leave to go home. From there, I reported for duty on a ship anchored in Brooklyn, New York — the USS Destroyer Kidd. I no sooner got on the ship and, the next day, I was reassigned to the USS Texas. It was an old World War I battleship, in Chesapeake Bay, Maryland. Twenty of us were sent there for gunnery school. I became part of the deck gang. I didn't like it, and figured if I talked about my electrical training at Coyne Electrical School, perhaps I could transfer to the electric department. It so happened the chief was looking for guys like me. I always prided myself on my ability to speak up and, this time, it paid off. I became part of the electric gang. My main job for quite a while was to obtain and show movies onboard.

What made the whole stint worthwhile for me was that I got to see a lot of places: South America, Newfoundland, Virginia, and through the Panama Canal to Hawaii. Pearl Harbor was gorgeous. I'll never forget it. There were so many military men there.

Then the Japanese came on the scene. One day as the sun was setting and I was sitting on a fantail on the ship facing the sun, we saw two planes fly right by us. "Oh, Christ," someone said, "there's Jap Bettys," Japanese planes.

We ran inside and turned on the battle station alarm. One fellow looked at me and said, "They're going right by us!"

We shot one of them down and someone else shot the other one. That was close! The Bettys came in through the setting sunlight so no one saw them. We wondered how they could do that. We had radar that was supposed to catch them before they came close. I guess someone was sleeping on the job. When they fly out of the setting sun, a favorite trick of the Japanese then, you can't see them until they're almost on top of you. When I saw them, I couldn't even move. I was like, "Where did they come from so suddenly?" But they weren't after my ship. They were after the carriers. I saw one plane that was shot down in the water. All that was visible was a wing which was on fire. This event changed me.

A young fellow next to me said, "You know, Gus, a guy could get hurt out there."

I agreed. I tell everybody that, at that point, I went from twenty years old to forty-five in my head. Everything became more serious, and I had an entirely different feeling or attitude about the whole situation.

Soon afterwards, I was sent to communications school in Washington, D.C. for the next three or four months. I was fortunate to be transferred to the States. Twenty-three days after I left the ship, it was hit by a Japanese plane, and I lost thirty friends.

My life has been blessed in many different ways throughout my lifetime. I'll tell you about them as we go along. I was especially lucky to get off the ship when I did.

When the war was over, I was honorably discharged. I returned to work with my father and spent the summers at Hart's Village with the family. My father bought a piece of property next door, and we started to build cottages, calling the property "Gustine's Cottages."

2

Asking Mildred to Marry Me

The Kaiser family had a cottage on the lake. One day I leaned over to check my boat and Mildred, a girl I had previously met, was on the dock with her friend. She pushed me into the water. I didn't know whether to laugh or get mad at her. We were hardly friends. I just knew her and she knew me. I remember saying to myself at the time, "This girl has plenty of spunk." It attracted me. I had been dating her friend back home in Meriden. Mildred invited her for the weekend.

Although I wanted to ask Mildred out, I couldn't because it would have put me in Dutch with her friend, and I didn't want a confrontation. So, I asked them both to go dancing at a local pub, the Ivy Inn. We all liked the music. It was good dance music, like Glenn Miller, Artie Shaw, and other big bands of the era.

We went to other nightclubs in the area that night, had drinks, and danced some more. Then I took them both for a tour of the neighborhood, which included a roller skating rink, a few hotels, dance halls, and nightclubs.

I didn't think of Mildred's friend as permanent. I knew something was missing in our relationship — that it wasn't going to last forever. I danced with her, and then I danced with Mildred. On the dance floor, I told her, "I think I'm with the wrong girl." She laughed.

Time passed, the camping season was over, and we were all back in Meriden. I didn't ask Mildred's friend out again. But, a few weeks later, I called Mildred and asked her to go to the movies. When I brought her home, I put my hands on her shoulders, kissed her on the cheek, and then said, "I'm going to marry you."

"You're crazy," she said. My friends wondered how I knew she was the right girl after one date. I told them, "I believe somebody was looking out for me."

We dated for about a year. Dates then were generally going to the movies and stopping afterwards for a hamburger or ice cream. Sometimes, we stopped for a drink, but we weren't really drinkers. One or two drinks were all we ever had. We spent time together visiting her folks and mine, and she really got to know my mother well.

Meriden was a jumping place in those days. Of course, there were no shopping malls then. The center of town was where the action was. We had big name family-type stores that were fun to go to like J.C. Penney's, Grant's, and Woolworth's Five and Ten. On Fridays, everyone went downtown. It was shopping night because most fathers were paid that day, so there was money to spend. I hanker for those days because today, thanks to shopping malls built out of town, city sidewalks are so empty. The malls pulled people away and eventually stores closed. What were once beautiful, busy cities often became like ghost towns.

I knew Mildred's family, especially her brother, Fred, and her father. I went hunting with them several times. Fred was in our so-called gang. We sometimes went out together for a beer.

Before I could marry Mildred, I had to get permission. I went to her mother and asked her if I could marry her daughter. That's how it was done in those days. Her mother was ecstatic because she knew my family and me. She predicted a long, good relationship between us.

Our marriage lasted a long time. In fact, it lasted fifty-three years! To this day, I say it was a marriage made in heaven, literally. We never argued in anger. Although, if we were mad about something, we discussed it, stated our opinions, and resolved the issues. People today find this hard to believe, since they tend to argue, raise their voices, and slam doors. Sometimes, divorce or separation is the outcome.

At the time we were dating, Mildred worked as a purchasing agent at a printing company in town, Miller Printing. Today, the company is out of business. She walked to work, rain or shine, since it was only about a mile from her house.

One day, as I was getting ready to go on a date with Mildred, my sister, Marion, asked me, "When are you going to break down and buy Mildred an engagement ring?" I think she had an ulterior motive because her husband's uncle owned a jewelry store in Massachusetts.

People kept things in the family then. "If you want to, we'll go up there and you can pick out a diamond, and it'll save you some money."

"Sure," I said. "Let's go." It was a Saturday night. I had a date with Mildred for seven, but at eight o'clock I was in Massachusetts. I called her. "Hi, Mildred?"

"Where are you?" she said. I think she was angry, although she tried to sound polite and at ease.

"I'm in Massachusetts with my brother-in-law on business. I'm going to be late."

"I'll be waiting," she said and hung up.

I said to the uncle, "You know, I don't know the first thing about diamonds." We could say that then, especially to a friend or relative. We knew we could trust them, that they wouldn't try to take advantage. I kept looking at the beautiful stones and wondered which one Mildred would like.

He told me the prices, the number of carats and all that stuff. He tried to educate me on buying diamonds, but I became impatient — impatient to be with Mildred, impatient to buy a diamond, and impatient to see her face when I presented her with it. Besides it was getting late.

We narrowed the selection down to six, but I still couldn't decide. My sister was no help either. She liked them all. I think she wanted her husband to buy her one, too.

The uncle was also becoming impatient, I think. He said, "Take them all with you."

"You mean it?"

"Sure. Have her pick out the one she likes and send the others back to me by registered mail."

I figured that was a pretty good idea. He wrapped them up individually in different colored paper, put them in a box that was similar in size to a box for chocolates, and we left. By the time we got back, it was eleven in the evening. I wondered how Mildred would react.

I was not prepared! I knocked on her door. She had been waiting alone for me all night. Her parents were out, and she looked angry.

I tried to ignore the look and said, as I tried to hand her the box, "I brought you something."

She was in no mood for a box of chocolates. That's what it looked like. "I don't want any chocolates," she said in a raised voice.

I always knew that if you give a woman a box with a ribbon on it, she's not going to be happy until she gets into that box, regardless of what is in it. So, as I was about to leave, I put the box on the dining room table and said, "This is for you. I want you to take it. I bought this for you."

She stared at me. The look could cut through glass. Silence. I said, "If we can't communicate now, I think the best thing for me to do is leave. I'm sorry I was late. I had business to do, and that's all I can tell you. I'll call you tomorrow and we'll start all over again."

Then, she looked at the box again. She took it in her hands ever so gingerly, like maybe she thought it wasn't chocolates, but a bomb. I don't know why, but her expression changed, and she carefully removed the ribbon and opened the box. Each piece was exquisitely wrapped. She opened one and exclaimed, "It's beautiful!"

I wanted to say, "Told you," but decided to just say, "You like it?"

"Love it," she said. "How did you know I would choose this one instead of one of the other chocolates?"

"Who said the others are chocolate?" I said as I smiled and laughed aloud.

"What do you mean?"

"Open another one."

She did. "Oh, this is even more exquisite than the other one," she said as she looked at the first ring which was already on her ring finger.

"Open the others," I said. Soon, all six rings were on her fingers. She began walking around, admiring them, like a woman admires her freshly painted fingernails. Before she could say anything else, I thought, it's now a different ballgame, right? Now she knew why I was gone.

She looked at me and said, "My mother will be home in about an hour. I'd like to have my mother..."

"Listen," I said. "It's not about your mother. Choose the one you like, because when I leave, I'm taking the other five with me. One is yours." I must say the rings looked good on her. One was a little diamond that was worth twice as much as the others.

In the store, the uncle had said, "Don't worry about the size even though it's small. It's a perfect gem." Another one was big and gaudy. He said, "People buy this kind when they're on the stage. It's a flashy stone. It's too gaudy, and it's the cheapest one. I don't think she'll choose it."

Mildred chose an emerald cut diamond which was beautiful on her finger! "I love this one the best," she said. So, it was done. She put the others back in the box and handed it to me. "I love you," she said as she wrapped her arms around me and gave me the best kiss I had ever gotten. Now, I knew she forgave me for being four hours late! A major argument was averted.

"Okay," I said. "I love you, too, and always will." I picked up the box and said, "I'll call you tomorrow and maybe we can go to that movie we were supposed to see tonight."

"Great idea. I can't wait to show my parents the ring."

"The ring is for you, not for your parents," I said and left.

It was summer. We set the date for our wedding for October 23, 1954. We were married in Meriden at St. Andrew's Episcopal Church, which is still there. We invited about sixty or seventy people, mostly family and friends. Afterwards, we had a reception.

We decided to drive to Florida for our honeymoon. On the first day, halfway down the New Jersey Turnpike, we got a flat tire. I said to Mildred, "Boy! I hope this isn't an omen for our future."

"Let's not even think about that, okay?" she said. We drove to the Jolly Roger Motel in Fort Lauderdale. It was a new place that was recommended to me. When we got there, there were twin beds in the room. "This isn't going to work," I said. We both wound up sleeping in one bed.

When we got home, we moved in with her parents because we wanted to save money for a house. Her mother said, "You can stay here until the summer and then move to the lake." We did that. In September we rented a cold-water flat in Meriden. It's where you furnish your own stove to heat your apartment. We bought an oil burner stove to cook on and it heated the apartment. We had a bedroom, living room, dining room, bathroom, and kitchen. It wasn't much, but it was okay with us, since we were saving everything we could to buy a house.

At this time I was working in New Haven with my father at the Haywood Electrotype Company. He was the superintendent and I was a journeyman learning the business, just as he and my grandfather had done before me. We made letterpress printing plates, an elaborate process in those pre-computer days. However, as time went on, the business went under with all the new-fangled processes that came out. It reminded me of the old blacksmiths who used to shoe horses to use for transportation. When the cars took hold, they went out of business, too. Then I went to work for another printing company as a purchasing agent. I made above average wages, which gave me some money to fool around with. I still wanted my own house.

3

Buying Hart's Village

Hart's Village, East Hampton, Connecticut

By now, we had four cottages built at Gustine's Cottages. I told Mildred that there was room for two more cottages, and that my father and I were going to build them. I also said, "Mildred, I'll take you any place you want to go, anything you want to do. But when the sun is shining, we're going to work on the cottages night and day, Saturdays and Sundays. That's the deal." We lived in Hart's Village, but she often came over to sit on the porch with my mother and watch us build. Another fellow helped us build the cottages. He laughed as Mildred came up the driveway. He used to call her, "The girl looking for a rainy day."

Mildred and I decided to wait to have children. I wanted to be sure we could live together and go forward, and that she could manage money. Once we accomplished those goals, I told Mildred, "We could think about starting a family." She agreed without hesitation. I wonder if I would have been so agreeable if she had laid her cards on the table.

At the time, I gave Mildred all my pay to manage our house. She enjoyed doing that. It gave her some responsibility and was fun for her. Meanwhile, since I didn't have to worry about money or anything else in the house, I could dream.

What Mildred didn't know was that I saved almost every penny I earned in the Navy. There wasn't much to spend it on. Most of my needs were taken care of, even entertainment in the form of movies. I could have spent it gambling, I suppose, but I wasn't a gambler. So, the money just stayed in the bank and accrued interest. I said to Mildred, "When Hart's Village comes for sale, I want to buy it."

"But, I want my own home," she countered. Every wife, in those days, wanted her own home.

Hart's Village came on the market. I told the owner, Cliff Abrams, we would buy it the next year. I knew that people weren't buying real estate since the market was down and no one had money. I thought it was a good bet that it would still not be sold by the time I saved enough to buy it.

Then, I said to Mildred, "A year from today, I'm gonna buy Hart's Village. It's for sale. I'm gonna work all the overtime I can." This was before the baby, so Mildred was still working and saving her pay. I put a mark on the calendar one year from that day. I saved enough money before the year was up, but I didn't want to appear contrary. Like I said many times, "I think the good Lord was watching over me all the time, like when He found Mildred for me."

I drove to Hart's Village. Cliff was still there. I said, "I've come to buy the camp." He knew I was interested and serious, but he was also adamant and upset that he hadn't sold it yet. Was this another instance of the Lord looking out for me?

Cliff said, "You made me wait a whole year. Now, I'm going to charge you another thousand for it."

"Well, I've got $500 in my pocket. Write me a receipt, and we're going to buy the camp."

I went home and told Mildred about buying the camp. She said, "Where'd you get the money?"

"I just happened to have it squirreled away."

"You lied to me."

"I never lied to you."

"You were dishonest."

"Call it what you may. I just didn't tell you I had it, that's all." I knew that if she knew I had $5,000 saved, she would have wanted me to buy her the house she wanted instead. But, I wanted to prosper, to invest money to make money. In the long run, that would make it easier financially to buy the house and go forward at the same time. I had dreams, but I knew they were realistic. I renamed Hart's Village "Nelson's Court."

It didn't take long for unusual things to happen at Nelson's Court. Early one day somebody said to me, "See that site in the back corner? The people who usually take it haven't been here for quite a while." Upon checking, I found out that they were gone for two weeks. Because we were so busy in the summer, we lost track of them. Also, I don't get involved in campers' personal lives. However, the two couples with their daughter came back and said that they went to Reno, Nevada. Each couple got a divorce and they married the other's spouse. The little girl was the flower girl for each couple when they got married. Everybody in the camp was shocked. My mother was especially so. She couldn't quite grasp that at all. She had problems even talking about things like that. They stayed with us for the rest of the year, seemed to be very happy together, and then they left. They did not come back again, so I don't know what happened to them. It surely was a strange situation and it became the talk of Nelson's Court for a while.

Now that I had Nelson's Court, we could start the family we hoped for. It took longer than we expected, but Mildred became pregnant! We were thrilled.

We were at my sister's house for Christmas dinner. Suddenly, Mildred turned to me and said, "You have to take me home. I feel funny." No sooner did we get home, when she said, "I think you should take me to the hospital," which I did. I stayed about ten minutes or so, got her checked in, and into bed. "You better go home," she said to me.

"You don't have to stay because you're not having the baby. I'll be okay." Like a good husband I went home and went to bed. In those days, husbands didn't even think about staying until the baby came or even being in the birthing room. By this time, it was about eleven at night on Christmas Day.

As I was leaving, I said, "Just give me a son, and I'll buy you a house." Glenn was born on December 26, 1959. To this day, I wonder what I would have done if he had been a girl.

The phone rang about two in the morning. "You better start looking for a house," she said.

"I'll be over soon," I said. I was ecstatic, not about buying the house, but about being a father. I waited a long time to start a family — and here it was.

When Glenn was a few weeks old, we started looking at houses. By this time, I changed jobs and worked in Bristol, Connecticut, about a forty-five minute drive from the campground.

Mildred liked a Colonial house we saw during one of our rides. It was on a pretty street and was her taste. So, on my way home from work every day, I rode around neighborhoods looking for the kind of house Mildred wanted.

One day, I went by the same house she pointed out a few weeks earlier — and there was a "For Sale" sign on it. My cousin was a real estate agent. I went home and said to Mildred, "Get my cousin on top of this, and if you like the house, we'll see if we can buy it." We hadn't been inside, so I wasn't sure it would be okay.

It was 1962. I went to the bank to apply for a mortgage. I told the banker, "I'm looking for a five percent mortgage."

He said, "The rate is five and one-half percent. Nelson, why don't you check with another bank to see if you can get one at five percent?"

I jumped up and I said, "My grandmother banks in this bank. My mother and father bank in this bank. My sister banks in this bank, and I bank in this bank. I'm the first Gustine that ever came here looking for a mortgage. What do you tell me? Go to another bank." I got ready to leave.

The banker was dumbfounded. He said, "Nelson, we're having a meeting at the bank today at one o'clock. I will present it and call you at three o'clock today."

I waited for his call by the phone. At three o'clock, the phone rang. "Nelson, you've got it, five percent."

One thing that was impressed on me years before was that the only thing the bank has to sell is money. My grandmother always said, "Most things are negotiable."

The house turned out to be fine with a school right up the street and a sidewalk in front. It was an excellent house on a boulevard. We only lived there, in those days, six months of the year because we were at the camp in spring and summer. However, it was our home. Five years later, on October 16, 1964, we were blessed to have our second son, Bruce.

4

Buying the Farm

Looking across F Area

One summer, one of our cottages that we rented by the week was vacant. A camping couple from Arizona came looking for a place to stay to put their trailer while they visited friends on the other side of the lake. I let them stay. They parked right alongside the cottage, and we provided electricity by putting a cord through the window and plugging it in. They were happy. They said they didn't want to stay in their friend's yard because they wanted to give him privacy and also have some themselves.

Two or three weeks later, when they were getting ready to leave us, I had a discussion with the husband. He said there weren't any campgrounds in the area. It would be a good idea, if I had any property, to start thinking about building a campground. A light went on in my head! It was probably the first time I heard the word, "campground." He said that he and his wife really enjoyed being with us. He told me he was an executive with a large Arizona insurance company, and they did a lot of camping. The people in the various campsites were always nice and friendly. He said, "When you are camping in a campground, and you invite your neighbors for a cup of coffee or a beer, people get into good general discussions. It didn't matter what we did for a living. When we were on vacation, we were just friends having a good time." He said it was something to look into. So, as I say, that was the first word that anybody mentioned to me as far as camping was concerned.

A farmer, who was doing a lot of work for me, had a small farm that was not doing too well. His family, who wanted to sell the farm, held three mortgages on it. He asked me if I was interested in buying it. We discussed the sale, and we managed to make a deal. I would pay each mortgage off, one at a time, and I eventually did!

It was quite a challenge to figure out how to afford it. I always dreamed of owning a large piece of land, I guess from my "cowboy days" when I was fourteen and dreamed a lot! I wanted a piece of land that I could walk on all day and get good and tired and still be in my own yard. We put our finances together and managed to buy the farm. At the time, I had a pretty good job and Mildred also worked.

Nelson's Court had about twenty-five to thirty campsites and two houses for rent also. So with all that, and the houses we had at Gustine's Cottages, we were busy in the summer!

After I bought the farm, my wife said, "Now, what are you going to do with it?" That was a really good question because I had no plans except to own a big area of land. The first thing that came up was, since it was an existing farm, it was on record with a division of the U.S. Department of Agriculture related to farming. A short time after I bought it, an agent from the department came to visit me. We discussed uses for the farm.

There was a program with the government where we signed an agreement not to grow corn on eight acres where the previous owner grew corn. I signed the four year agreement, and received a payment from the government to not grow corn.

The agent said there was a federal program to help build a pond on the property. The government paid me $500 to help build it.

Also, the agent suggested growing Christmas trees. He explained that we could obtain small Christmas trees from the federal government, plant them, and after ten years when they grew big enough, sell them. It sounded like a pretty good idea, but that would use all the land, and I would not be able to use it for anything else because it would be full of trees.

A footnote to the above is that many years later I did receive some free Christmas trees. The Conservation Department gave me about four hundred or five hundred Christmas trees at one time, and I couldn't find time to plant them. One day a camper saw the trees and said, "Would you like me to plant them for you?"

I said, "That'd be great." He asked me where to plant them. "Plant them on the other side of the Rec. hall," which was then a large area. And that's what he did. Two or three weeks later the grass was about twelve inches high, and I forgot about the trees. I purchased a used riding lawnmower and, of course, everybody wanted to run the lawnmower. Another camper volunteered to cut the grass in a big field and did a good job. Then, he decided to be a good guy and cut the area next to the big Rec. hall where the grass was also quite high. So that was the end of my Christmas trees in that location.

At that time, I was working and had a good job as a purchasing agent at a printing company. I got to talking about camping in general with some of the men that worked there. I found out a camping club in the area just started. One of them said to me, "Gee, you ought to go join the camping club." Actually, I found out there were four clubs like that within a range of thirty miles or so. Some were just getting started. So, we joined several camping clubs. They had meetings in the winter. In the summer, we visited different campgrounds, but there weren't too many of them. There were some magazines about camping. One was the "Campfire Chatter." People interested in camping bought these magazines to learn where the campgrounds were.

One of the biggest problems we encountered before we started the campground was the fact that the local zoning regulations had nothing pertaining to camping or campsites. When regulations don't exist, it can be difficult because the committee members are reluctant to let anyone do anything that the members don't know anything about. At that time, there were two boards, zoning and planning. Today, in East Hampton, there is only one combined board. I took a chance and called the planning chairman, Russell Dart, and told him I'd like to come down to see him. We had a good chat about what I wanted to do. Since he had time on his hands, he came out and walked around the property with me. He thought it sounded like a pretty good idea, and it would be good for the town. The campground and the farm combined were one hundred and forty acres, which was quite large, and he saw that the town could increase the budget with the property taxes collected from it. Although houses could be built on the land if we wanted to, Mr. Dart felt the campground/farm would be a bigger asset for the town because there wouldn't be additional children for the school in town. He agreed to work with me to try to put a zoning law together. It took about two years, but he did it.

At the same time I was trying to start my camping business, another fellow who lived not too far from us was trying to build an airport. This was in 1964. There was a lot of controversy about it. But, he finally got approval. In the airport zoning regulations, there was one sentence that said, "Recreational use of land is a permitted use in a rural area." I hadn't put it together when someone called me to say, "Hey, here's your chance. You can apply within that regulation." So, I checked it, and went to see my attorney to tell him what I wanted to do. I asked him to come to the zoning meeting with me. He said, "No, you don't want big guns and stuff like that. You just put on your dungarees, your cowboy hat, and your boots. Then go down to the meeting and tell them like it is, one boy to the other. You'll be better off like that." So, that's exactly what I did. I went down and presented my case. The next day, May 27, 1964, the headline in the "Middletown Press" newspaper was "Trailer Camp Site Approved." The first paragraph read, "The East Hampton Zoning Commission approved the application of Nelson Gustine for a trailer camp site on Mott Hill Road Tuesday night at the town hall. Renewal must be sought before May 15, 1966." The application was for a two-year permit.

The next paragraph said, "Gustine plans to operate the camp from May through October, and it will not become a permanent trailer site, but a camping site, he stressed."

People at the meeting who were in favor of it urged its approval because, at the time, Connecticut lacked campsites. It would be good

---

Wednesday, May 27, 1964

Trailer Camp Site Approved

EAST HAMPTON, May 27 — The East Hampton Zoning Commission approved the application of Nelson Gustine for a trailer camp site on Mott Hill Road Tuesday night at the town hall. Renewal must be sought before May 15, 1966.

Gustine plans to operate the camp from May through October, and it will not become a permanent trailer site, but a camping site, he stressed.

Among those who spoke in favor of the proposed camp site were: Walter L. Pratt, state director of National Camping and Hiking Association; Erwin Kelsey, Middletown, state soil and water director; and First Selectman Helge Palm.

Gustine plans to open the camp with 40 sites, and if it progresses well will have upwards of 120 campers. Both Kelsey and Pratt urged that it be approved as Connecticut lacks campsites, and establishment of a site here would increase the number of sites in the state.

Reprinted with permission from The Middletown Press

---

for Connecticut to have them.

The two-year renewal didn't mean much to me at the time. I was just happy my request was approved! I couldn't wait to go back to my lawyer with the newspaper to show him the article. I said, "I took your advice and, boy, I got it!"

The attorney looked at it, wrinkled up his brow, and threw it into the garbage can. He said, "What do you think you're going to do with that campsite after two years and they don't give you another permit? The Supreme Court sticks up for the Zoning Board most of the time, so you have to be careful." It was like he cut the legs right out from under me. However, Mr. Dart of the Zoning Board had been working with me. I figured we'd start so we did. I figured at the end of the two years, we'd have more knowledge of what we were doing. So we applied for a permanent permit two years later.

The first thing I needed to do was drill a well. The well-digger I hired needed to get on the grounds with his truck, but we had no real road into the campground. I got a price of $2,200 to bulldoze a road. It would not be a fancy one. We needed to knock down trees and remove rocks so we could drive in. It seemed like an astronomical price at the time, to just bulldoze and make a rough-graded road. At that rate, I thought, I'm going to be broke before I begin! I thought, maybe I should buy a bulldozer and build the road myself!

My brother-in-law was a mechanic. When I told him I was going to think about buying a bulldozer, he laughed at me because he knew that I didn't even know where the spark plugs were in a car, let alone know how to run and maintain a bulldozer! But, I was persistent and wanted to try it. He had a friend in the business, and we went to see him. He had a TD9 'dozer, which was an international one that was quite famous then, but is now obsolete. I bought it.

We started to build the road. My father-in-law just loved getting on the bulldozer and playing with it, and he did a lot of work for me because he was retired and had time, while I was still holding down a regular job. He was a great guy, and I loved him very much. We had a lot of good times together.

I paid $2,300 for the bulldozer, $100 more than the original estimate to have a contractor build the road. We also needed it for other things, including the pond, which we built later. The bulldozer was probably one of the best investments I ever made! We lived to see the day we literally wore it out!

Bulldozer for clearing the land

After we built the road, we had the well dug, so we had water. We installed a few spigots here and there for potential campers to use. Then we built a half-dozen dry pit toilets (outhouses) and scattered them through the grounds. There was electricity to run the pump, but none for the campers.

We were new to camping and wanted to get the word out that we had campsites. We printed brochures and flyers, which we kept in our cars. Wherever we went, we left a few at gas stations, stores, and wherever people could see and take them. This caught on as did word of mouth. People first came by themselves or with their families. The next time, they brought friends with them. That's how the business grew.

The original office

One camper, an older woman, was down at Nelson's Court. She had a tent, and thought camping looked great. She moved her tent up, and she put a sign on it: "Office. Knock for Attention." This was our first office. It was like a comedy. How do you knock on a tent?

We didn't get a lot of campers because, at the time, there weren't too many people who knew about it, or were interested in it. It was still a novelty. It was very much in the rough, so to speak. But, we did get some people. Often, they asked, "Where can I camp?"

I just said, "Well, we have one hundred forty acres to camp, so go camp wherever you want to. I would suggest you camp someplace close to a bathroom." By that time, we ran lengths of water pipes to strategic areas to make it more convenient for the campers. The first year, in our eyes, was successful. We didn't break any records, but at least we started!

After we were in business about a year and a half, Mr. Dart discussed the proposed permanent zoning law with me. One regulation in the draft was that there were no restrictions as to when camping could take place. It could, in effect, be year-round. He was reluctant to allow this because people might think I was going to create a mobile home park, which people wouldn't like. He re-wrote the regulation to include a clause that camping would be permitted from April 15th to October 15th, which was fine with me. He also wanted to include a clause that some camping could be done in the winter, especially if we were going to build a pond. We might even like to use it for ice skating parties, etc., he suggested. We added a clause that would allow for campers to stay for a month in the winter, but had to maintain their permanent address because they could not live in my campground. Actually, I had no intention of doing anything in the winter anyway, but it was good to have the legal possibility.

When the zoning law was to be acted upon by the committee, close to two years after we received permission to begin, my family and I went to the meeting. One thing I impressed upon everyone was that we had been in business close to two years. I said, "Not a single person has found any reason to complain. We did nothing to disturb the neighborhood." Over the years, we were always conscious of the neighborhood. If we played music, it was not too loud for the neighbors because we laid the campground out down in a valley. However, when we play music, we always stop it in the evening at eleven sharp. This worked well throughout the years. I treated the campground like it was my personal home and kept it the way I like my home to be.

At the meeting, no one came up with a reason for the law to fail. Someone could have objected on the grounds that they didn't want a campground, but that wouldn't have held much weight. What would their reason be? No one came up with a reason. The law was approved, and it served us well for the past forty-eight years!

A footnote to the airport: One night several years later, late at night, there was a very heavy fog. A plane flew over the campground. We thought surely it was going to crash in the campground but it didn't. Evidently the pilot didn't have a flight plan because the people from the airport were in the campground looking for the plane all night. It created quite a commotion. Later on, we learned that it crashed in the state forest. I don't think anybody was hurt.

5

A Conversation with Mildred

Nelson and Mildred Gustine

Camping was something that didn't really fascinate me in the beginning. When I was a young girl, my family used to go to the park for the day. We had a campfire and a cookout. This was my first exposure to camping. We walked in the woods quite a distance. It was ideal for us.

Nelson asked me to give up my job at Miller Company after Glenn was born to take care of him. I said, "Nelson, with your job, we could manage and I am happy to take care of Glenn." The campground was growing and I was alone while Nelson was working in Bristol, Connecticut. Nelson always worked at the camp in the evening and weekends, so my job was to take care of the office and our son. I went from a forty-hour-a-week job at Miller Company to sixty-five hours a week at the campground. I got tired, but I did enjoy it.

Glenn and Bruce came with me to the campground to spend time with Nelson while I fixed the meals. It was hard because we were "roughing it" at the campsites. It was not like today. Today it is sophisticated. It's different. Some probably still like the roughing type of atmosphere. That's true camping, a place without a stove in the house.

I did tell Nelson, "If I am going to go camping, I want a stove that I can cook on because I'm not building a fire and having two little kids running around." I built some fires for the meals in the beginning. We survived. I grew to kind of like it. I liked being outdoors. It didn't bother me so much.

We eventually got a trailer to set up at the campground. It was hard because then I was running two houses, so to speak. There were times where I felt, "You're crazy, this is too much."

Things just seemed to evolve. It was one thing after another. "Honey," I said to Nelson, "I'm doing things I never did in my life. Hey, wait a minute," I said to him, "For better or worse. This seems for worse with all that we have going on."

Glenn, Mildred and Nelson at their campsite

Time passed and the kids started going to school. So, during the week, I couldn't go to the campground at all. I couldn't take them out of school. Nelson went down to the campground. I stayed home in Meriden with the boys and cooked meals for the whole weekend.

On the weekend, the boys and I headed to the campground since I had a car. I had to have one to get around. We all at least spent time with Nelson as a family, usually working.

Nelson couldn't find the time to go on vacation while we were building the campground. There was always a project to do. However, early one fall, Dolly Lawrence and the children decided to go to Florida. They asked us to come with them. I said, "We are all going. We would like you to come with us, Nelson." After several discussions, Nelson was persuaded to go. Although Nelson saved vacation time at work, he intended to use it to build the campground, but this time we went on a real vacation. All of our children were at the right age, and we all needed a vacation. We had a great time.

As the boys matured, they became workers and got paid something like ten dollars a weekend. They were thrilled with the ten dollars. Then I said, "You know, you're stealing. You should be ashamed of yourselves." Well, I started low because I knew they were going to ask for a raise because they were digging ditches, and putting in poles, and helping with many things.

My father did a lot for Nelson. He liked that because it gave him something to do. I was afraid it would cause trouble with my mother but, no, she was good about it. Once in a while she sputtered because she needed things and he couldn't take her shopping, so I would. Nelson and my dad enjoyed working together on the campground projects.

In the early 1980s things were busier, as we grew and grew. I said to Nelson, "Nelson, you better retire from printing. I need your help."

In 1981 Nelson told his boss he wanted to retire. The only trouble was that George, a good friend of his who was the comptroller, had put in for a raise for Nelson of $1,000. Nelson came home and said, "I can't retire. George already put me in for a raise for $1,000." So Nelson didn't retire right away.

A few months passed and things kept growing, so again I said, "I don't care, you have to retire. I need you, and I need your help here." Again, he went to George and told George the same thing. The first thing George said was, "I just put you in for another $1,000." Nelson did get the raise, so he didn't retire that time either.

In 1982 I told Nelson, "I don't care about the money, I need you." He went back to George and said, "I don't want any more raises, I'm going to retire. Mildred really needs help."

So in 1982 Nelson retired. I know he enjoyed his work with George, but the campground was really getting quite busy and I needed his help.

6

Building the Campsites

There was a big demand in the beginning for gravel and fill to build the campsites and the roads. I was very fortunate to have an area where gravel was in the camp. The big problem was moving it to where I wanted it. I owned a truck, and my father-in-law, who just retired, liked to drive the bulldozer. That year we spent most weekends in the fall moving gravel to what eventually became campsites. I hauled the dirt down and dumped it. Then he spread it and made the campsites look the best that he could. It worked out nicely.

By the end of the fall, we couldn't go down to the campground because by the time I got out of work it was too late. The weather was not very good on the weekends so, to not waste time, I decided to build some more picnic tables in my garage that winter. I made them in sections, and later in the spring, I brought them down to the camp and reassembled them. At least I kept busy during the winter.

But, I really needed more picnic tables. At work someone told me about a man in Bristol who started to build a campground but never finished. There were fifteen tables at his site that were for sale. I contacted him and made a deal to purchase them. Bristol was on my way home from work. I stopped every night to pick up tables. They were put together with bolts, so I took them apart. That way I could take two tables at a time in my station wagon. When I took them to the camp, I reassembled them.

Future site of the dam

Clearing the land

One of the first situations we dealt with was the lack of a phone at the camp. We lived in Meriden in the early days and went to the campground on Friday night. We had a phone in Meriden with a message recorder on it. That was the telephone number that we used for the camp because we didn't have a telephone there.

One man took a walk up in the back end of the campground and he kept going. He walked through the forest and wound up in Portland, which was a long walk. His thinking was he would keep walking in order to reach the highway where he could probably find a telephone. He did just that. He found a telephone and called my campground number. The only trouble was, when he called the number, he got the answering machine in Meriden. His idea was to call the campground and ask someone at the camp to tell his wife to come to pick him up. He left a message on the recording. He was pretty disgusted, and I'd like to tell you what the message was, but I don't think it would be very nice to put it in print. Once we were established we, of course, put a phone in the camp office.

Then there was the challenge to name the camp. I liked the idea of

Cutting stone

Building the road parallel to dam

Digging a well

The front gate

calling the camp, "Nelson's Family Campground." Our fee was based on mother, father, and unmarried children living at home. One family came one time with six children. They talked about beating the system. They told me they really liked the 'Nelson Family' part of it because we charged by the family, whereas most camps charged by the person. They owned a station wagon, and whenever either the husband or wife drove out of the campground, he or she would holler to the other one, "I have two and you have four." They never called the children by name. It sounded kind of funny, but they did that all the time.

Nelson's
Family Campground sign

7

Building the Pavilion

We needed a pavilion, a place where campers could gather. As seemed to happen with me, a fellow approached me. He said he liked to build things and could build anything. "Give me a free campsite up there," he said pointing to an empty lot, "and I'll help you build a pavilion." His name was George Hall, and he was a heck of a nice guy. Since he could use the land for free, I wouldn't have to pay him to build. Besides, I didn't have much money. I agreed to supply the materials. Together, my father-in-law, the kids, whoever else would volunteer, and I began to build. Hall was the chief engineer, and I had veto power. Now that we had our first building up, we decided to use the front part for the office and store. It is now the laundry area.

In the front half, which was partially open, we ran a crafts program. Mrs. Dunphy would corral the children and motivate them to paint, draw, and make things. We had stuff all over that the kids made. It was wonderful. I thought that we were really in business now. All the business and activity was centralized around the building. This worked out for quite a few years.

When the camp was only about a hundred campsites, I could not get vendors to deliver soda, ice, and other things that we needed. At the time, we used part of the office as a store. I owned a station wagon. Coming home from Bristol where I worked, I went by an ice house. Often, I stopped there and bought ice blocks and cubes. To this day,

Arts and crafts in the pavilion

I'm surprised I made it back to the campground before they melted. I purchased a freezer, so I brought them back to the campground and put them in the freezer. I bought sodas at a wholesale place and also carried them in my car to the campsite. Later on, after we had the Rec. hall store, deliveries became a different story. Dealers

The pavilion store

became willing and happy to come into Nelson's, even with their great big trailer trucks.

In the beginning, when we first had a small store in the pavilion, we kept track of income and transactions on a small adding machine. It was inconvenient and time-consuming because we had to figure out and make a separate entry for the sales tax on each purchase. At the end of the week, it was a big job for me to take all these adding machine figures and try to make sense out of them so I could get a total of what took place. At one of the conventions we attended, there was a vendor who sold cash registers. We bought one. We replaced it several times over the years. It totalled all the sales, separated the sales tax, and came up with a number for the sales tax. At the end of the day, we got a take for all the transactions for the day. At the end of the month, we got a printout of all the transactions for the month, which was not only efficient, but also convenient for us.

One of the first things that I did was purchase a movie projector. Every Saturday night I showed movies, mostly cartoons for the kids. I obtained free films from companies that used the movies to sell their advertising. I put up a sheet for a screen so they could see both sides of the screen. Everyone came to the movies. If it rained, everyone was underneath the roof. In good weather they were in the road watching from the other side. But if a car went by, we had to shut off the movie until it left.

One Saturday night we were getting ready to show a movie, but it wasn't dark yet. A woman came to me and told me that there was a skunk under her deck. I told her to leave it alone. She was not very

Movies at the pavilion

happy with my answer. Then she asked several boys to pick up the end of her deck so the skunk could escape from underneath. One of the boys threw a stone at the skunk, and the rest was history. The skunk sprayed the whole area. It was so bad I didn't think there was any way we'd have a movie that night. I knew that it was better to use vinegar instead of ketchup, which is always messy, to eradicate the smell. I bought a gallon of white vinegar and stored it in the shed. I also had a bug sprayer I used to spray for mosquitoes. I mixed some of the vinegar with a little water and put it in the bug sprayer and sprayed the area. It was almost like magic, as the smell disappeared quickly. Later the whole gang came and we had movies that night. I couldn't believe it.

8

The Quonset Hut and the Last Outhouses

There were several outhouses throughout the campground that needed to be replaced. They couldn't remain permanent fixtures. The reasons follow below.

In the early days we had several dry pit toilets scattered around the campground. There were two in B Area, one for men and one for women. There were also two in the tent area with the same designations.

One night, my wife and I were visiting friends in B Area when we heard a woman scream. It was dark, so my friend and I grabbed a flashlight, and took off to see what was going on. The woman was completely panicked. It happened that when she used the outhouse and was partially undressed, she saw a flash, a light coming out of the dry pit. Thinking there was somebody or an animal down there, she screamed and flew out of the outhouse. We finally calmed her down. I found out later that a woman who used the bathroom before took a flashlight with her and put it down beside her. When she got up, the flashlight rolled down into the dry pit pointing face up and lit. By the time the second woman came in, the light was dim, but it still flashed occasionally. The next day the woman was a lot calmer and laughed about the whole episode.

Another time, a woman went to the tenting area to use the bathroom. When she sat down over the dry pit, something flew underneath her and hit her rear end. She yelled and screamed, then flew out of the outhouse not realizing she did not pull her underwear up. A bunch of children saw her and laughed at her. We figured there was probably a bat in the pit. When the woman sat down, she covered up

The last outhouse

The Quonset hut foundation

the hole so the bat couldn't get out. It kept flying around trying to find a way out. Every time it attempted to get out, it hit her rear end. Not knowing what was happening, she panicked also. We knew we had to give serious thought to building a building to house flush toilets.

At the time, we were living in Meriden. There was a large park in Meriden that held thirty or forty military domed Quonset huts that were built and used for housing during World War II. One owner wanted to sell his. We went to look at it and decided to buy it for about $250, which was a good price. I hired someone to take it down with the idea of putting it back up at the campsite. When I went to see what he was doing after a half a day, I noticed that he was about to demolish it! I fired him! My father-in-law and I took a claw hammer and started taking it down. It was all big sheets of corrugated metal. We numbered each one as we removed it so we would be able to put it together correctly at our site. The farmer that I bought the campground from had an old truck, which he brought over, and we piled all the metal sheets on it to take them to the campground.

It was our last day in Meriden before leaving for the camp for the summer. My pregnant wife and I followed in my car. As we drove through Middletown and Portland on the way to East Hampton, the Portland police were conducting a large-scale inspection program to find unregistered vehicles. While the farmer drove right through, I was stopped, and when I couldn't produce an updated registration, we were arrested for driving an unregistered vehicle. The police took us to the courthouse in Middletown. I had American Automobile Association (AAA) Insurance who posted a bond for us. It wasn't much money. The police said they would call a wrecker to come and pick us up with the car to go to East Hampton. That was where we were headed. It was supposed to come in twenty minutes. The policeman just left us at the side of the road, outside the courthouse. After an hour, nobody came. I said to my wife, "We can't stay here all night. We'll just keep moving." That was a mistake! About three miles up the road, there were flashing lights all over the place. The police stopped two or three other cars because there was an accident. It looked like we were driving right into it. We pulled over to the side of the road. I had my field glasses with us, and I looked out the window. I saw the same policeman who ar-rested us. He was directing traf-

Building the Quonset hut

fic. "Oh no," I said, "We're going to be arrested again." So, we just stayed on the side of the road. A wrecker came and cleaned up the area, and the policeman left. As soon as we saw an opening, that is, it was all clear, we drove on. We arrived about two in the morning in East Hampton. That was some lousy night!

The sides going up on the Quonset hut

The next morning we took on the project of dealing with the Quonset hut. First we dug a foun-dation for it, and then put some plumbing into it before we reas-sembled the hut. Piece by piece we nailed it back together, thanks to the foresight of coding it when we took it down. The hut was too long, so we removed a few sections and put them on the other side of the campground for future use. Today, one is a storage building and one is an additional bathroom. If things were different then, I probably would have constructed a differ-ent type of building. At the time, it was clean and neat, and it served the purpose. There are three toi-lets and sinks on each side and four showers. It is one of six bath-room buildings that we now have on the grounds.

We were quite happy when

One of Nelson's sons working on the Quonset hut

The Gustine's take a break while working on the Quonset hut

we had flush toilets and showers. Soon we found, on several occasions, that since the showers were free, people used them to wash their dishes. I received quite a few complaints because, when people washed their dishes, it left a residue from the dirty dishes in the shower. Also, they would let the hot water run like there was no end to it. On several occasions we ran out of hot water, and people complained about that, too. We found a solution to this problem at a campground convention, a coin machine to operate the showers. After we bought and installed the coin machine, we never had another problem.

Since the building was quite wide, we kept a four-foot space in the middle to divide the unit into the men's and ladies' rooms. We constructed a wall that was about seven or eight feet high, so it didn't reach up to the ceiling. We figured that it would be okay because the space above the wall would enable air to circulate throughout the building. What we didn't realize was that boys can be mischievous!

One day, one of the campers came to me and said, "You know, there are some boys in the men's room. I don't know what they're doing, but I think you better go and check on them."

I ran down to the men's room. I didn't see anybody when I entered, but as I walked further into the building, I saw two boys sitting up on the top of the wall overlooking the ladies' room. Of course, they were up there watching and checking on the girls going in and taking a shower. When they saw me, they panicked! They knew they were caught. I got them out of there and grounded them. They were not allowed to roam around the campground for the next two or three days. It didn't take long for the story to make the rounds of the campground. Luckily, no one got hurt. I thank God for that because the peeping Toms could have fallen down into the ladies' room!

Another time, a female camper reported to me that she smelled smoke in the bathrooms. I ran down to see kids sitting on the con-

crete floor. They took toilet paper, bundled rolls together, and
burned them. Kids do get some
funny ideas. These kinds of things
made me a little nervous.

Once the Quonset hut building was up, Mil and I took turns
cleaning it. It was my turn. I first
checked the men's side, then went
to the women's side. Before I en-

Mass at the campground

tered, I always knocked several times on the door. I would also holler,
"Is there anybody in there?" There was no reply, so I went in. There
were doors separating the shower room, so I knocked on that door
several times. No answer. I went in. To my surprise, there was a
woman there who just got out of the shower and stood there in her
birthday suit. I was shocked and so was she. I hurried outside. In
front of the women's door was a man laughing when I came out. It
turned out to be the husband of the woman in the shower. He continued to laugh and said they were from Canada and his wife didn't
understand a word of English. I left feeling much better knowing that
the husband thought it was so humorous.

The second half of the Quonset hut we put up remained open, and
there was a lot of junk in and around it. There was a family in Area C
whose relative was a Catholic priest between transfers. They invited
him to stay with them for a week or two. They told me everyone in
Area C would go clean up the hut if we let the priest say Mass. About
thirty to forty people gathered, and after Mass he took up a collection.
This happened two or three times. One of the campers liked the idea
of having a Mass at the camp. She went to the local priest and asked
him if he would come up every other Sunday and say Mass for us.
But, he cut her down to size by saying, "If you want to go to church, we
say Mass in town once every Saturday and twice on Sunday morning.
You all come down to my church." The camper was disappointed, but
that's the way it was.

After the bathrooms were in place, we decided to knock down and
burn the old outhouses. The last two that needed to come down were

Award ceremony celebrating the last outhouse

in Area G. We sent some boys up there to do the job. When Al Brilliant, my friend and camper, saw what was going on, he said, "You can't knock this one down because I just had it put into the historical record. It's registered with the federal government and it's a crime to destroy federal property." It became almost a joke. So, he decided to take care of it. He cleaned it up and put a chain around the entrance. He had a sign made that declared it a federal historical property.

Al made a really big deal of this, and everyone laughs when they hear the story. This is the last outhouse still sitting up there, but, of course, it is not in use.

9

Horses, Goats, and Chickens

An interesting thing took place years ago. A camper, who had an important job at a bank, was looking for a place to stay for a short time. His daughter was into show horses. He walked around the campground and then came to me. "Do you own all that property up at the other end?" he asked me.

"Yes."

"Why don't you build a building and go into the horse business up there?" This really intrigued me because I liked horses. I watched the cowboy movies with John Wayne then, and I still do today. But I'm not one to jump too quickly into a scheme, so we kept talking for a while.

"I'll bring in someone to run it for you," he said.

"Okay, bring him down and I'll talk to him."

Sure enough, the following week when he came to camp, he had a fellow with him. I think he came from either Peru or Chile in South America. He wore authentic-looking South American clothes: hat, boots, and pants. It looked like he just got off the boat.

We got to talking. He was a horseman. He spent all his life with horses and said he knew all about them. He could buy, train, and sell them. He said we could make a lot of money.

The banker invited me to, "Come to the bank and let's talk about it."

I would be the first one to say Mil did get a little upset, especially when I talked about having horses in the campground. But that never materialized. I went home and talked to Mil about the scheme. She was convinced I was going to do it. She knew I didn't do things too fast. I make sure everything is going to be all right before I delve into something. So, she said to me, "I've done everything I can to be helpful to you, to work with you, but I'm going to put my foot down now.

I'm not going to shovel you know what!"

"Okay," I said in a very loud voice. The neighbor across the street in one of the cottages later asked me if I was having trouble with my wife.

"No," I said. "She just got a little excited, but it's all water over the dam now."

A few days later the banker, horseman, and I met at the bank. The banker explained that I'd have to take out a mortgage to build the building. I was reluctant. The horseman sounded convincing, though.

"The only problem I have is if I borrow money, build the building, and buy horses, you might decide to go back to South America," I said, looking at the horseman. "I don't know anything about horses, and the risk is pretty great. The only way I see that we can work this out is you gotta post a bond. That way, if you decide to take off, I got some money to work with," I finished. No decision was reached that day.

But the fellow from South America wouldn't give up. He came back two or three times to try to convince me to go through with it. Finally, I was able to convince him that I wouldn't take the risk, I didn't have the money to gamble. He finally left.

Someone in the campground always knows something about what's going on. One day somebody came up to me and said, "Are you going to do business with that turkey?"

"No," I said.

"Well, you're lucky because he got fired at two places where they train horses because he's supposed to be a great trainer, and I guess he is. He is known to know about horses, but he spends too much time with the women. He's looking for a job."

"Thanks a lot," I said. "Why didn't you tell me that in the beginning? I wouldn't have gone so far with it."

The horse idea wasn't over, though. A young girl who lived on property bordering ours used to ride a horse. She would ride down the road to visit friends. One day, her mother came to me and said, "Would you let my daughter ride through the campground? I get nervous when she rides down the road."

"Sure, no problem," I said. She rode through a few times. We weren't too busy at the time. She was a nice, polite, young girl.

Then, one day, Mil was taking a walk on the grounds. Another woman came onto the property on horseback riding a horse pretty fast down the center green. They jumped over a picnic table. Mil became excited but, by the time she could catch her, she was down in the B Area, at a sort of dead-end road. The horse did its business right in the middle of the road. Mil said to her, "You have to get off the horse and clean up like they tell you if you have a dog."

The woman said, "Oh, I don't do that. I thought you did that."

I think someone told her she could ride here because we let that young girl in. However, Mildred told her, in no uncertain terms, that it was the last time she could ride a horse on our grounds. We never had horses here since.

Another animal story is about a goat I bought. In the winter, we had no place to house him. A friend of mine, a lumberman who did some work for me, offered to take it for the winter.

The following spring, he brought the goat back and said, "I'm not sure, but this goat got out in the neighborhood during the winter. There are other goats in the neighborhood." The goat cut herself on a piece of wire and had a big gash, so I took the goat to the vet and said to him, "Tell me if this goat is pregnant."

"Goats are not like women, goats are very difficult," said the vet. He wrestled the goat to try to get her into position and told me, "No, I don't think so."

There were a couple of campers who were doctors' assistants. I asked them the same question. One of the assistants tried to examine the goat with a stethoscope. He said there was a little farm in there — it wasn't like listening to a baby's heart. There were all kinds of noises in the belly. He said that the goat wasn't pregnant. But, the next day, there was a little goat wandering around.

The neighbor said it got to be quite a conversation piece that winter. "Everyone likes babies," he said.

Then he said to me, "You want some chickens?"

I said, "Yes, give me 'em."

He said, "Just put them in a fenced in area, and they'll stay there. If you feed them, they'll fly, but they'll come back."

So, we had three chickens. Unbeknownst to me, one of them was a rooster. At six o'clock every night, they all flew up in the tree to roost. In the morning the rooster came down, got on the fence, walked down to our campsite, and perched near our bedroom. At five thirty, we would hear "cock-a-doodle-do." That was funny for a while. Campers thought it sounded beautiful. However, one woman behind us, who got out of work about one or two in the morning, was not too happy about being awakened a few hours later. She complained to Mildred, who would literally put her feet against me in bed at the sound of the rooster and push me out of bed.

There was a Korean War Veteran in the campground. I said to him, "I gotta get rid of that rooster. Now, you can't get a hold of it, you know, you just can't catch it."

He said, "You want me to shoot him?"

I said, "Okay, but you gotta be careful."

The Korean War Veteran got his gun, and that was the end of the rooster.

One of the campers said to me, "We'll take the chickens from you and we'll have a nice chicken dinner." I let them have them because the novelty of the chickens was wearing off by now.

Regular animals could also be a challenge sometimes. A couple that had a tent trailer had a dog, which they left in the trailer while they went to work. This was already a bad omen. During the day it got so hot in the tent that the dog became panicky. He started shredding the canvas to pieces until he finally got out. He was running wild around the campground and the kids were chasing him. They yelled so everyone could hear, "Mad dog, mad dog, get out of the way, mad dog." We called the dog warden, who came and told everybody to stop chasing the dog because that kept him riled up. The warden asked for a dish of water. When the dog walked by, he drank some water and then settled down. That was all the dog needed to calm down. When the owners came home, they were surprised about their dog's behavior. The dog warden was waiting for them.

Nelson's goats found a way out of
their pen and came to visit

10

Gold in Them Thar Hills?

Gold in East Hampton Hills

EAST HAMPTON (UPI) — A geology professor has struck gold in the hills of eastern Connecticut, but he says the vein is probably not extensive enough to send people rushing to the woodland rivers with pans.

Anthony R. Philpotts, a University of Connecticut professor of geology and geophysics, announced his discovery Monday after verifying that the mineral deposit he found Memorial Day weekend was definitely gold.

Philpotts was conducting a field work course on Meshomasic State Forest land in the Cobalt section of East Hampton when he discovered what he believed was gold mixed in with quartz and iron pyrite, or fool's gold.

Reprinted with permission from The Middletown Press

A family moved nearby when we first started the campground and stayed most of the summer. The husband was a trucker who owned four or five ten-wheel trucks, which are pretty big. He hauled feldspar, a mineral used for sweeping compounds and ground up for other uses, although I never learned exactly what. He hauled the feldspar from Portland to Middletown, Connecticut, to a processing plant. When the drivers were finished for the day, they used to drive up to his campsite to have a beer with him. He noticed that we had some feldspar that was coming out of the ground in one area. He said, "Gee, that's what they mine over in Portland. You could sell that."

I said, "Well, that sounds interesting."

"Tell you what," he said, "I'll tell my boss and have him come." A few days later he came, I showed him where the field was, and he quickly identified the feldspar there.

"What are you going to do with the property?" the boss asked me. "They tell me you're going to have a campground there."

"That's right," I said. "That is our intent, and that's what we're going to do."

"Well," he said, "I think what you ought to do is get a rocking chair and set it out in the yard, and you let me mine the feldspar. You just count the trucks driving out of the yard, and you don't have to do anything but add up the trucks carrying the feldspar out."

"Well," I said, "that sounds pretty interesting. I'll talk to my wife and let you know."

My wife said, "That sounds like a pretty good idea."

I'm the kind of guy that has to follow everything through to the bitter end whether I do it or I don't. I have to know everything about it. I talked to my father-in-law. He said, "Let's take a ride over to Portland to see what it's all about." We drove in and there was a mountain there, practically cut right down the middle.

It was pretty obvious that if you take a truckload of dirt out, you leave a hole. When I realized that, I said to my father-in-law, "That's not for me. I don't want to do anything like that. That's worse than planting the Christmas trees. I can't do anything, and they're destroying the property." He agreed with me, so, I nixed that idea.

When I was thinking about writing this book, I came across some history about East Hampton, Connecticut. According to a diary written in 1787, the President of Yale University talks about Governor Winthrop of New London. He tells of how he was told that Winthrop and a servant went into the woods and mountains for a few weeks. They melted ore down and made metal rings. Land records in East Hampton support this legend because several pieces of land are entered in land records as the "Governor's Ring" lots.

I learned that there were other accounts of gold being found. I wasn't surprised that one of our camping families believed that gold was in nearby hills.

An interesting young fellow came to the campground. He was a caretaker in the 5,000 acre state forest that bordered our property on one end. There was a hiking trail there, and it was his job to keep the trail open for hiking. About this time, there was an article in the newspaper about Cobalt, a section of East Hampton which is about ten miles from us. Some college students went to Cobalt to rummage through an old mine, and they discovered gold. The headlines in the newspaper read, "Gold in East Hampton Hills."

My wife said, "Now, that sounds like the best deal of all."

So, off we went to Cobalt to check it out. The gold was found in the rocks immediately above the rocks that contain cobalt. Since it's state land no one is going to be digging it up looking for gold. Besides, most of the gold was removed with the cobalt.

A fellow came to us asking if we'd let him grub stake. He wanted to look around the property to see if we had gold. Nothing ever came of that idea either, but it was interesting how people thought and what they wanted to do.

11

Big Al

One of the most memorable characters to come to the campground was a man known as Big Al. He came for three summers with his wife. They were from Florida, and he was a bulldozer operator, working on Connecticut Route 2 at the time. I owned a TD9 'dozer, but didn't know much about running it. I could push dirt and back grade it, but being an amateur bulldozer operator, I couldn't make a level floor.

We got to talking, and he told me he drove a bulldozer every day. He drove a TD9 when he was a kid living on a farm in New York. He got onto my 'dozer and began working on Area B where we were planning to build another campsite. I could tell he was good. He knew what he was doing. He was a little crude but his work impressed me. He did a tremendous amount of work on the pond.

One day when I was with him, we got to talking to some of the other campers. One of them said, "Do you work here?"

"No," he said.

"Do you camp here?" the camper asked.

Al said, "I pay to work," meaning he was paying me for the campsite and also working on it. I think it was his way of pushing me. By this time, I was totally convinced that he knew what he was doing because he already helped me a lot. From then on, I never charged him to camp with me.

One year, my bulldozer was leaking a lot of oil. Big Al said, "We have to take the darn thing out and fix it once and for all because we have to keep putting oil in."

I had to agree with him. Al said, "Dig a hole with the backhoe and drive the bulldozer over it. Now you can get underneath the 'dozer."

My father-in-law and I dismantled the motor from the 'dozer. I got the backhoe, picked up the motor, and put it on the ground so he could fix it.

The trouble was that Al was a drinker. He didn't drink only one drink at a time. No, he drank several straight whiskeys and did not stop. Then, when he was drunk, he went into his trailer. It was at the end of the season, and I hadn't seen him for a few days.

Al's wife came over to me and said, "Nelson, I can tell you something right now. When Al wakes up, he'll be so sick, he will quit drinking."

I knew he drank a lot because there were several quart bottles in their trash. I couldn't understand how one person could drink all that. His wife said, "When we got married, he got drunk on our honeymoon, and he was drunk for a whole week!"

I said, "That should have told you something."

She didn't comment on what I said, but did say, "I can tell you also that when he drinks, he don't care about nothing. When he finally wakes up, the first thing he's gonna say is, 'Pack our bags. We're going to Florida.' So, if you want anything done with your bulldozer, you better do it now."

It was a Sunday and my father-in-law was also at the campground. I told him what happened. He was puzzled, but he helped me hook up the tractor and put the motor back in the bulldozer and it remained like that until the next spring when Big Al and his wife came back.

Although I would have liked to offer him a drink to celebrate his return, I knew better. He did a lot of work for me that season. I had a cow pasture loaded with rocks. He worked hard to clear it. He even tried to beat me down to get on the 'dozer. He arrived before me. He planned it so that he could get on the 'dozer before I came. He did a lot of work without my even asking or suggesting he do it. If he saw something that needed to be done, he just did it. Where the pool would eventually go, one weekend he decided that we should push the dirt from one side to another along with the rocks and everything else and make a big pile. It took all weekend. When we were finished he said, "Get the backhoe and dig a big trench." After I did that, he said, "I will take all the rocks and move them out, throw them down the hole and I'll 'doze it all clean." What a great job he did!

Then he extended the length of the blade. Now he had two more feet on each side of the hole. After all the dirt was pushed back it looked beautiful. We then seeded the area.

Burying rocks

Big Al had his own personality. One camper who was with us for several years erected an Indian teepee and did a lot of entertaining. For some reason, Big Al didn't particularly care for him. One day Al was out in the field trying to bulldoze it clear, but the bulldozer was drowning out conversations that this particular camper and others were having. The camper asked me to get after Big Al. I went over to Big Al and said, "Al, they're trying to learn something about Native Americans down there, so let's move to another part of the field."

"Are you trying to build this darn campground, or do you want to listen to Indian stories?" Al asked.

I had to give in. I said, "Okay, keep going." I didn't want to upset Big Al who was working so hard for me.

12

Building the Pond

The Department of Agriculture came to talk to me about using the land, including planting Christmas trees, as discussed before. They also suggested building a pond. The deal was that the government would pay $500 to help with some of the cost. The best thing to me was that they would secure all the permits, would have their surveyors survey the site, and constantly check with me as the pond was being built to be sure it was being done correctly. The pond was to provide water for wildlife and farm animals. We decided to go ahead with it. There was a brook running through the property. At the time, the water was hardly running.

The agent said he would send surveyors in. They would look for the two highest points in the campground to help determine where to build the shortest dam for the pond.

Good Friday of 1963 was a gorgeous, sunny day. The representative from the Department of Agriculture came to the campground to discuss the plans for the pond with me. I met him where I thought the pond should be built. He told me right away that we couldn't build the pond there. "It is the most expensive place you can build a pond because there's only one high point. We have to build the opposite end up high, and that means an awful lot of fill."

His surveying crew suggested the pond be built at the other end of the camp because there were two little knolls, and between them a dam could be built. "It is the shortest distance on top of the knolls, and would make the shortest dam." He also said if we built the pond between these two knolls, it would flood the neighbor's yard by about 150 feet!

That didn't sound too attractive to me. I said, "I don't want a pond there. I'd have to get an easement from the neighbors. That means I gotta give them an easement to use the pond. I don't think going forward is a good idea."

He reminded me, "If you build the pond where you want it, it will require an awful lot of fill."

"Like I said," I told him, "the pond is only good if it's where I want it, so this is where it's gonna go if we're going to build it." Finally, he realized I was going to get my way or not build at all, so he agreed! Then he said that we had to cut all the trees around there in three different areas in a straight line so the surveyors

Pond sites and center of pond

could see with a surveying instrument. This meant five hundred feet of trees, which were growing quite densely. "You don't have to take them out," he said, "just cut them down so the surveyors can see with their instrument. When you get done, call me and I'll send a crew in," he finished.

By this time, it was about eleven in the morning. It was getting cloudy, although it didn't look like it would rain anytime soon. My father-in-law and I came directly from church to meet the man from the Department of Agriculture, so we had our dress clothes on. I had my chainsaw in the truck. My father-in-law said, "Well, what are you going to do, just sit here and look at it?"

I said, "No, I guess maybe we should start cutting." That is what we did. We kept at it, cutting the three areas so the surveyor could come back and do his survey.

At noon, we were still cutting. A thunderstorm gradually moved in at three in the afternoon. We were still cutting even though it was raining hard. The brook had about a foot of water in it, running really fast. We heard hollering and a horn blowing to get our attention. We didn't realize the time. I said to my father-in-law, "That sounds very much like your daughter."

He replied, "No, I'm afraid that sounds more like your wife!" She was blowing the horn. My mother was after her because we didn't come back for dinner. We were quite wet. I guess my wife figured it

This was not planned

out because she soon met us at the campground with drinks, sandwiches and dry clothes. When she saw what we had done, her mood got better. I think she felt a little sorry for us, being wet and all.

Monday morning, I went to work. From my office, I called the department and told them we were all set for the surveyors to come down. My contact laughed at me. "You mean, the trees are cut down, all of them?"

"Sure, you said cut them, so we did. But, we didn't remove them."

"That's all we need, just so the surveyor can see a straight line." The next day or day after, he sent the crew down and they re-surveyed the whole area. About two weeks later, the maps were ready.

Now that I was about to build the pond, I had to clear the area with a bulldozer. I decided to clear the area for the dam with my TD9 bulldozer. I knew that sooner or later I would need a larger 'dozer. At the end of Big Al's second year, he took off for Florida. After he left, I found a big 'dozer parked where we wanted to build the dam for the pond. I didn't know where it came from, and, I didn't know how to run it. It just sat there. I knew the mystery would have to be solved, but I didn't know when. Sure enough, about ten days later a man came to me and he said, "Are you building a pond here?"

I said, "Yes, we are trying."

He said, "I think you have my bulldozer." After talking about it for a while, I believed it was his 'dozer. Big Al had been working on Route 2 nearby. I later learned he knew someone who owned the equipment company that rented out bulldozers. He rented the 'dozer for me and had it sent over. The problem was that Big Al never told me about it, and he was the only one who knew how to drive it. As I said, he left for Florida. So the man took the 'dozer out. I thought the idea of renting a 'dozer was great, but unfortunately Al didn't stay long enough to use it.

As we were just starting to build the pond, an agent came in from the Connecticut Fish and Wildlife Department. He had a complaint that I was going to block a trout stream. I asked him to take a walk down to the brook with me, and he did. I wanted him to see that there was no water running in the brook. He checked the brook and left saying, "No problem, thank you for your time." That was the end of that.

The pond site

When Big Al came back the following year he never even mentioned the 'dozer. By this time, we were ready to finish the pond. The Department of Water had a big 'dozer that they rented with a driver or without. I rented it, and Al started to work with it. Then we found out we needed two 'dozers so we could work faster because the water was coming in. I rented another 'dozer with an operator. With the two 'dozers, we built the dam in almost a day — and avoided a flood.

The next day they leveled the area off. We already put in an overflow pipe to run underneath the dam. Once the water entered the pond, the overflow pipe underneath the dam took care of any excess water. That's the way it is today.

Then I planted grass on the dam itself. When we finally saw the water going down the overflow pipe at the dam, it was a happy day for me.

It turned out to be a two-acre pond, which we still have today. There is fishing, swimming, and boating on it. There was a raft in the middle. It all worked out great for us.

A funny incident happened when we were actually digging out the pond area. Some of the kids found a turtle about fourteen inches in diameter, which was a pretty good size for a turtle. I told the kids to put it back in the brook and they did that. Not too much time passed when another kid brought it back to me. This happened maybe three or four times. Finally I decided to buy a can of yellow paint to identify it if it should surface again. In small letters I put on the turtle's back "NFCG" for Nelson Family Campground. The kids still kept picking it up and bringing it back. When the water was in the pond, we put the turtle in the pond. Later on, it seemed like the turtle disappeared because we didn't see it for a while. After a few weeks, a man came to me and he said, "Hey, there's a dead turtle with yellow markings 'NFCG.'" Unfortunately, somebody killed it so it was just laying there with "NFCG" painted on it. Somebody must have thrown a stone at it. Kids are always doing some mischief.

Bulldozing the pond

Once the pond was completed, we used it for swimming. For security at the pond we had one rule. A camper had to be accompanied by someone fourteen or older, and no one was permitted to swim alone, which made sense to me. Although a lifeguard was not legally required, when the beach was crowded, I always had somebody there to make sure adults were with their children. On several occasions mothers would get upset because their children had taken swimming lessons and they thought it was okay for them to swim alone. I couldn't concede to that. I insisted on several occasions saying, "I can't have anybody swimming down there alone, and even though he's a good swimmer, you have to have somebody with him." We have not changed the rule. Today we still live with it.

To make a beach at the pond, we put two loads of sand on the ground. Mildred lent me the money to buy two paddle boats. I told her it was a non-interest loan. Of course I had to repay her.

I built a floating raft in the middle. The kids enjoyed the floating raft. They all got on one side. It would make it tip so everyone would fall in. The raft lasted a few years because people were swimming around it at the same time the kids were trying to tip it. It looked very dangerous to me, and I was always afraid people could end up getting under it and getting hurt.

After a few years, I decided to remove the floating raft and make a new stationary raft because I feared somebody was going to get hurt on the floating raft. I drained the pond. I dug four holes to put four telephone poles in position. I had to wait for the pond to freeze and then I purchased planks needed to build the raft. We had a problem because it snowed and the lumber truck could not get close to the pond. The lumber truck dropped the material just inside the gate, and it was a long walk down to the pond. We got some rope and tied

Building the raft in the pond

each one of the planks individually. We all took turns and pulled. It wasn't very hard to pull them because it was on the snow. We were all holding onto the rope and walking down to the pond pulling one of the planks. Mil said it was like working in China. With the help of my wife, my sons, and a few of their friends, we managed to get all the planks down to the correct position. Once we had all the planks down to the pond, we began to build the raft. It was easy because the ice was the right height so I could construct the raft. We got the whole outer part done and some of the top of the deck. The wood that we didn't use was put on top of the raft so we could finish in the spring. It was nice because the ice kept everything in the right position so it was easy to work.

I was very pleased with the results with the raft. We did a good job and it got plenty of use for about twenty or thirty years.

The pond in the late 1960s

One cold winter, the pond froze over pretty solid and the ice raised two of the poles creating an unsafe situation. We drained the pond and dug alongside the telephone pole until it settled into a level position. That idea worked fine, but the next cold snap it raised the raft up again. This happened three times. The last time was in 2010. It raised two of the four poles up a foot high. We decided we couldn't work with it and we had to remove the raft because the kids would get out there and somebody would slip and get hurt. The raft was removed. Today there's no raft in the pond.

Thank God we have the pool.

After we built the pond, we decided to stock it with trout, which I did several times. A camper was camping close to where the trout were put in. As he was leaving, he told me, "This is a great campground you have here. I paid $2 a night to camp," the rate at the time, "and I've been eating fish the whole week." I found out later from the hatchery that every day they feed the fish at about the same time. Every evening these fish jump up all over the pond. The camper found this out and was right there to catch them.

The youngsters seemed to be trying to fish all the time. We held a contest. Whenever a young boy or girl caught a fish, he or she could come up to the store to register it. Whoever caught the largest fish that month entitled the family to a free weekend at the camp. Since then we had fish stocked in the pond, but we did it at night when nobody else was around.

Car in the pond

One day a young boy said, "Mr. Gustine, somebody drove their car down into the pond."

I said, "What are you talking about?"

"Come down and see," the youngster said. Sure enough, in D Area, somebody parked his car on a little hill and left the car in neutral. The car rolled right down into the pond. I had to get my tractor and pull it up.

Most of the time, everything ran smoothly. However, we did have a casualty at the pond. A young boy was with his mother at the pond, although I later found out the mother could not swim a stroke. The boy was prone to seizures. While swimming to the raft, we believe he had a seizure and drowned. I was at work when I received the news. Because I built the pond and the family was in a very close group camping with us for several weeks, I knew this young fellow quite well. He always wanted to ride in my truck with me. His death had a big impact on me. I was not right for some time.

There have been several other deaths in the campground. We lost two men who had heart attacks. A young girl who babysat for my grandchildren, camped with her family seasonally for several years. At the beginning of one of our seasons, she came to the campground all alone. The next morning, friends came looking for her. They discovered she died inside of her camper from what we believe was carbon monoxide. It was a very sad day at Nelson's. Everyone loved her. She was such a nice, pretty, young girl.

Her family and friends planted a tree with a small plaque in her remembrance here at the campground. Each year they come to the campground on the anniversary of her passing to honor her memory.

Postcard of the pond

13

Insurance Rates Only Go Up!

After we lost a young boy in our pond, the following year the insurance company raised our rate a lot. The policy became effective in April, which was when we opened the campground for the season. I had no time to go looking for a new policy from another company, but I needed a policy right away. With that in mind, I purchased a seven month policy. That gave me time to check other companies when the policy came due.

One of the campground associations I belonged to was working with an insurance company that was very competitive. Seven months later, I changed to the new company.

Everything went well for a time — until the main company decided not to insure campgrounds. Quite a few campgrounds were left high and dry. In the meantime, a new company called Evergreen was being organized. It only insured campgrounds and was run by campground owners, which sounded great. I was impressed with the new company. When my policy came due, I changed to Evergreen. Evergreen has been very stable over the years. Today, it insures quite a few campgrounds. I'm very pleased I changed to Evergreen.

14

A Welder Saves the Day

Quite a few things happened while we were building the campground. It is hard to explain what made them happen. The only way I can explain some of these things is to say that, "Somebody upstairs is looking after me."

One fall day, my father-in-law and I were at the far end of the campground. There was nobody in the campground because the camp was closed. We just finished working with our bulldozer, when the bulldozer chain broke. We knew if we tried to drive the 'dozer, the chain would fall off. We needed a welder to weld the two pieces of the chain together so we could put the bulldozer back in the barn and secure it for the winter. The season was over, so we didn't plan to come back for a long time. We were just standing and looking at it, kind of like, "What a foolish thing to happen to us." It was a Sunday so we knew we couldn't call a welder to come out that day. We were discussing what just happened. I looked toward the entrance of the campground. A truck was pulling in that looked like it had a welder on it. Since I wasn't exactly sure, I walked toward the truck to see what the driver wanted. He was looking for a place to camp. I said, "Before you get into that, what's that machine you've got on the truck?"

He said, "It's a welder."

I said, "Do you know how to use that?"

"Oh, yes."

"Come with me," I said. Together we went back up to the bulldozer. I said, "Could you weld a bead on there so I can get that track together?"

He said, "It'll take me about two minutes." He welded the chain, and we drove the 'dozer down to the barn to store it for the winter.

I said, "What can I do for you?"

He said, "I'm working in the area and I know you're closed. There are no facilities. I'm looking for a place that's safe to park."

We had a cable across the road with a lock on it. I said, as I took a key off my keychain, "Here's the key to the lock. The only thing I ask is when you leave you lock the gate. When you come in and when you go out lock it so nobody comes in the back end. You can stay for one or two weeks, I don't care. I am so grateful that you came along when I needed you. You made my day."

Like I said, I think somebody upstairs was looking after me.

15

The Well's Storage Tank

Nelson Gustine standing alongside his water tank

My first well served me fine. It was at the beginning of building the campground. However, by the time we installed flush toilets, I knew we were going to need more water. That first well had iron in it, so rust developed in the toilet bowls. It was not very attractive at the time, even though we kept scrubbing them.

In 1971, I decided to drill a new well about three hundred feet deep on top of the hill which is now E Area. That way, water would run down by gravity to the Area B campsite area. Everything leads to another problem. The first thing we knew we needed was a storage tank. Somebody told me that there was a scrap metal dealer in Hartford, Connecticut, who had several tanks. I went to see him. He showed me a 20,000 gallon tank that was going to be used in a housing complex. It was painted inside with paint that met health department code. He had papers to prove it. Then the town finally gave the contractor permission to use the town's water so he didn't need the tank, so he sold it to the scrap dealer. I purchased it for $2,500,

Truck delivering the big tank

I believe, delivered to my campground. The next week, when they delivered the tank, I happened to be there. Two fellows came with a trailer truck with the tank on it. "We're looking for a spot to drop the tank," one of them said, "We were told to drop it in the first big open space."

Thank goodness I was lucky enough to be there. I told the boys, "I want the tank up close to the top of the hill where I'm going to use it. If you do that, I will buy you the best dinner afterwards."

One driver said, "I don't know."

The other driver said, "Let's do it."

They got three-quarters of the way up. Because of the weight of the tank and the trailer, the truck could not pull it. The wheels kept spinning. I got my 'dozer to try to push it, but I couldn't. So I said, "Okay guys, you did your job, dump it off here and I'll handle it from there." They were very close to where I wanted it and with our bulldozer and logs, we managed to roll it and get it up in the proper position where it is today. It cost $25 for two dinners.

16

The Garbage Challenge

You don't think of all the things that need to be addressed when you begin a campground. The first one that occurred was the challenge of garbage. Only weeks after we started the campground, it became obvious that we had to have a way to get rid of garbage. What would we do with it?

We decided to buy a dump truck to haul the garbage away. We found one for $350 that was good enough to register with the State of Connecticut.

We gave everyone a plastic bag that they filled and left at the site when they went home. We then drove the truck around and picked up the plastic bags. This worked out well for a while. It was a problem, of course, when the raccoons dragged the bags and opened them.

We decided what we needed was some kind of containers. So I waited for a sale. One of the stores had thirty-gallon galvanized containers. I bought thirty of them and sprinkled them throughout the campground. I asked the campers to place their plastic bags in the container near them. That way, we kept the cans cleaner longer. Of course, we had to go to pick up the cans. There was a lot of clunking and banging, and occasionally someone ran over a can. A few times, we even saw one in the back of a camper leaving the campground! The cans eventually became a problem. Especially as we grew, the amount of garbage grew also. As we became busier, we couldn't always get to the dump in a timely manner. Not everyone put the garbage in the plastic bags, even though we asked them to. People don't always do what they are told to do. The cans and the grounds became messy. So, we had to come up with another plan.

We worked out a system where we went around the campground and picked up the garbage a few times a week. On Monday or Tuesday morning, we took the garbage to the local dump. This worked out pretty well.

We then rented two dumpsters and placed them strategically on the grounds. Campers were supposed to put their garbage in plastic bags that we provided as a courtesy. Some even brought their own bags.

We never had any trouble getting help picking up the garbage because the guys used to love to ride in the truck around the campground. The kids, particularly, looked forward to getting in the truck. They picked up the garbage. They were really helpful when we built up the camp business.

A weekend camper came to me and said that he had a small compactor on his truck for garbage. "I'd like to make a trade-off with you," he said.

"What's that?"

"How about if I camp here weekends for free, and I leave my truck parked here? You'll fill it up with garbage. I'll take it to the dump because I have to go to the dump first thing when I leave Monday morning anyway."

"It sounds good to me." He parked the truck, and the deal worked out perfectly for me for about a month.

One day, a seasonal camper who owned a trucking company that hauled feldspar from Portland to Middletown, approached me. He and his drivers would occasionally come to visit at the end of work, sit, and have a beer while their big trucks just took up space in the parking lot. They talked about how they ground up the feldspar and used it for something, but that there was a waste by-product that looked like sand. I said to them, "You guys have a heck of a lot of nerve driving over here, parking in my campground, and enjoying a bottle of beer or two. The least you can do is bring me some of that sand." The next day four trucks came with sand. We made an instant sandy beach with it!

It was kind of comical to watch it. He had about five guys on the truck. Some of the electric wires that ran across the property were too low. He had to have one of the guys sit on top of the cab to raise the electric wires so the truck could go under them.

Then the camper suggested that he could get all our garbage disposed of efficiently. He proposed to bring one of his ten-wheelers to the campground on July Fourth weekend when we had the most garbage. In fact, at one time we had up to fifty garbage cans, which we had to replace at least once a year because they would get run over by cars, or, as I said, were taken home by campers when they left. I made the deal with him, and he continued to take our garbage throughout the summer into the fall.

Later that fall, Mil and I received an invitation to a seminar at one of the local trade schools. We met one fellow who stood up and said, "Gee, I think the camping business would be a really good business to get into. I heard of a campground that picks up its garbage daily with a ten-wheel truck."

Some people said, almost in unison, "That's a lot of garbage."

Mil said to me, "What the heck is he talking about?"

I said, "He's talking about us, Nelson's Campground, on the Fourth of July weekend when we had that big truck."

That man who stood up didn't know my camp or me. It was quite comical hearing them all talk about my garbage being picked up by a ten-wheeler.

When we got back home, we decided that the dumpsters weren't in good locations because they were too close to the campsites. We parked them closer to the entrance, and we asked everyone to place their plastic bags in them as they left when the weekend was over. We were recycling way before it became as popular as it is today. We had three dumpsters: one for bottles and cans, one for cardboard, and one for waste. Inevitably, someone threw the wrong bag in the dumpster. The next person followed suit so, by the end of the day, all three dumpsters were filled with garbage.

We always had a challenge to overcome. Years later as the business grew and the camping population increased, the grounds around the dumpsters got pretty messy with overflow or animals getting into them at night. Eventually, we rented two large compactors, and this worked out well. One is for recyclables and one is for trash. Campers just put the garbage in it. It compacts it — so it looks like there's practically no garbage at all! We also try to control the bottles and cans.

The grounds are cleaner. When people arrive or leave, all they see is the metal compactor, which is expensive, but it serves the purpose well. Today we don't have garbage challenges. We've got the dumpster with the compactor. When it's full, we call the dumpster company and they pick it up.

17

Camping by the Rock

For a few years we had no map to guide campers to where they could park and set up camp. Most campers drove in and parked at a spot that they liked. In fact, once a gypsy group came in and camped behind the Quonset hut. They liked it because it was a wooded site and a bathroom was there. Other campers discovered it and often called to say, "We have to go into the gypsy area because it is convenient."

Giant rock in D Area

Another popular camping area was the D Area overlooking the pond. A huge rock that was left over from a glacier was there. People wanted to camp in this area because from the big rock they could look up at the clouds and down at the view. It was a pretty spot. Also, the large rock was in the central part of the grounds, so campers could easily be directed to that area. Trouble occurred when children climbed the rock to the top. One girl fell off and sprained her wrist. Another fell off and hurt her arm. Since then, though, there have not been any accidents there. Once someone painted the rock, and I did not like it. I called the family to ask them to try to remove the paint. They did.

The life of the rock was doomed when we decided to build the Rec. hall. I hired a contractor to crush some smaller rocks to give us more room to park beside the hall. Then I said to him, "See what you can do with that great big rock in D Area." He managed to break it into a bunch of pieces, which we buried somewhere else in the campground.

People were still camping anywhere, so the campground did not look neat. One family came from Wisconsin. The father was taking summer courses at a nearby college, so the family came for several years. His young son was studying mapmaking in school. He saw we didn't have a map of the grounds. He asked my permission to draw a map of the campground to show where everything was located. I thought it was a great idea. He did such a great job that we still use part of his map today. Later on, we added the pool, miniature golf, and other new things, but the basic map is still hanging in the Rec. hall.

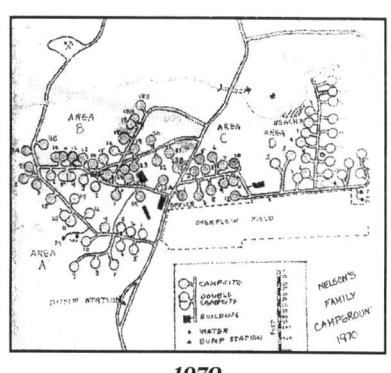

1970

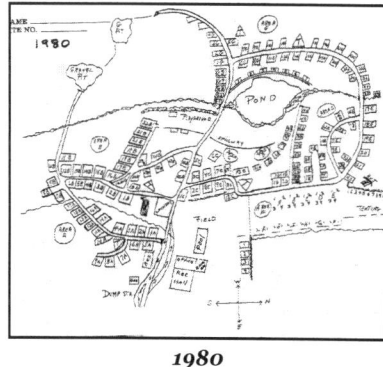

1980

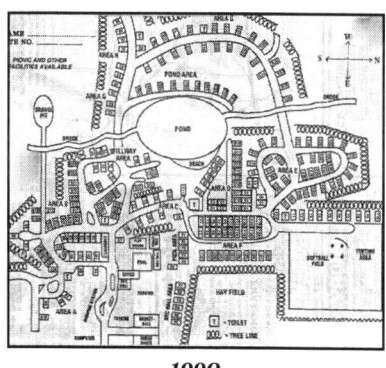

1990

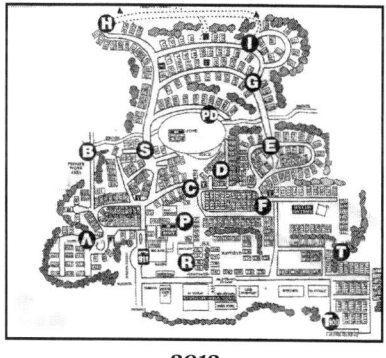

2012

Nelson's Family Campground maps

18

Hunting on Private Property

We had a lot of land that wasn't being used, so we decided to allow hunters to come during the hunting season. This was after the camping season was over, so it did not create any problem with campers. However, anyone who wanted to hunt had to ask me for permission. When they did, I said, "Okay, as long as I know where you are." I told them where to park so I could see their cars and know someone was hunting.

Connecticut had a program that required me to sign papers allowing hunters on private property. The state put up signs that read, "Permit Required." Then the state "stocked the land." That is, they put birds on the land for the hunters to hunt.

The rules or laws were pretty clear for hunting. No hunting was allowed within one hundred feet from any building. During hunting season, we worked the land and felt safe because, first, we saw any cars approaching. Second, we would ask to see their permit to hunt. This all worked well for several years.

A few years after we began to allow hunters to hunt, we put a small trailer on the land and spent weekends there. One day Mildred was in the camper. A hunter came by, saw a bird and fired at it. He was about twenty-five feet away from the camper.

My wife was scared half to death. That was the end of permitted hunting on the property. I sent a letter to the State of Connecticut to remove the signs.

19

Local Kid Trouble

When we first started Nelson's Family Campground, it was sort of a novelty for the kids. A lot of neighborhood children used to come over. Most of the time, they behaved pretty well and we didn't have any problems with them.

We had a lot of rocks and minerals on the land. Collecting them was a big hobby in the beginning. Today, most children aren't so interested in rocks. However, we had a huge hill that I decided to dynamite so the children could get to the hill. I hired a man from the feldspar quarry, who did the job. Now, the kids could go up there and look for quartz and other rocks native to our area. That first year, rock collecting was a novelty. Rock collecting clubs even came to explore.

However, as time went on the novelty wore off, and the local children became more rambunctious. We decided it might not be a good idea to let them come at will, so we told them politely that we didn't want anyone coming into the campground to play.

Another problem resulted from this. We had a sign out in front that said "Nelson's Family Campground." Over it I built a roof with a 4x6 to make it look cute and inviting. I didn't put the sign in concrete. It was just dug into the ground, so to speak. Therefore, anyone could easily pick it up and move it. One time, I got a call that it was down in Sears Park. The bigger kids probably took it in a truck. We then realized we might have more trouble. So we made the sign more permanent by digging a hole, encasing it with sections of iron and pouring cement into it. Then we placed the signpost into the ground. It hardened and the structure was more permanent. Since then, we have had no trouble with anyone removing the sign.

However, one night I noticed a bullet hole in the sign. One of the boys up the street was then very much involved with guns, but I didn't know it at the time. There was a hole a quarter-inch in diameter in the sign, and I wondered what the heck happened. I saw the light shining through.

Another time I noticed another hole in the sign. The first hole looked like it was shot with a .32-caliber gun. The second hole was larger, shot with a .45-caliber gun. It looked about the size of a quarter. At the time, I didn't know who committed the crime.

We decided we had to keep people out when we weren't there or when we were just working on the grounds. I put a cable across the entrance, and someone almost got tangled up in it. So, I decided to make the cable more noticeable. I took a fifty-gallon drum and painted it yellow. I took an axe and chopped a couple of holes in it, and then I ran the cable through the drum and put a lock on the other side. It may have been corny, but it served the purpose. Everyone could see the barrel.

About a week later, I came down and saw from a distance that the barrel was gone. I said to myself, "What the heck happened to the barrel?" The cable was still there, but no barrel. As I got closer, I noticed that the bottom of the barrel sat on the ground, and pieces of it were all over the place. It took a lot of strength to do that kind of damage. Later, a neighbor told me she heard the bang and then a car flew up the street. She knew which kids did it, and told me. It appeared to me that someone made a bomb which exploded. There was literally not much left of the barrel. This was the last destructive act of those kids. I think they're grown up now, and perhaps they're robbing banks. Who knows?

Sometimes, I just had to take things into my own hands. Every night after dark I walked around the camp to ensure that the teenagers were at their campsites. One night it was very dark and I didn't have my flashlight on, although I had it with me. I got down to the end of the pond where the dam is, and it was very, very dark. Of course, I knew my way around, but it was still pretty dark. I tripped and fell as I stepped on a young boy and girl having sex near the top of the pond. I turned my flashlight on to see who it was and, of course, I knew the boy and the girl. They took off like two jackrabbits. The next day I felt I should tell the girl's mother. When I told her, she became quite upset. She immediately changed the subject to talk about other kids doing things in the campground which had no bearing on what I was saying. I said, "If you don't have enough interest in your daughter's behavior, then I guess I don't have to have an interest in her either." I left. As I went around the corner of the trailer the father, who was sitting there, apparently heard every word that I said. I didn't know what he might do, but he got up, shook my hand, and thanked me. He said, "I'm sure it won't happen again."

20

Flooding

Every time it rained in the campground, water rushed across the field and went across the roads. In several instances the road eroded. It seemed that I was continuously trying to fix it.

Campers were very helpful. One of them saw me working on the road. He suggested that I go to the town dump to get some hot water boilers. He said, "Cut the ends off and use those for water to go underneath." I did as he suggested. There must have been a lot of problems with boilers that year because, believe it or not, I found four and loaded them into my truck. Then I went to a welder, and he cut the ends off. Each boiler was about twelve inches in diameter and about five feet long. I put them under the road and they worked out quite well for a while. But being only twelve inches in diameter, it wasn't too long before they started filling up with dirt. The flooding situation was becoming hopeless. I was frustrated.

When I was repairing one of the units, a camper came by and said, "You need a bigger concrete pipe."

I said, "I know what I need, but they're very expensive."

The camper said, "How many would you need?"

I thought he was kidding. I said, "Oh, maybe about thirty."

"Where do you want them?"

At the time I did not take him seriously, but answered anyway, "Put 'em out in the first field." The guy laughed. That was on a Sunday.

I was living in Meriden at the time, so Sunday night I went home and usually came back a couple of times during the week. When I returned one day, there was concrete all over the first field. There were more than thirty-five pipes. I later found out that a big trailer truck came and dumped them. All of the pipes had cracks in them and broken hubs, so were not salable by the company that was making them. People wouldn't buy broken products. The following Saturday

I looked for the camper in the camp and thanked him. He said, "Don't thank me, I thank you."

I said, "I don't understand."

Then he told me that he worked where they made the pipes. "In the handling, some crack and pieces of the hubs fall out and we cannot sell them. They keep piling up in the yard. We are always looking for a place to get rid of them. We used to put them in the dump, but we were filling up the dump so the town stopped us from dumping them." I was really surprised. We had enough pipes to put pieces under all our roads that were a problem with the water.

I think somebody must have been looking after me. It's another one of those cases.

21

Animals as Campers

I was in B Area working when a camper came one day with his wife and a young girl about thirteen or fourteen years old. They had a small trailer and found a site near the bathroom where they stayed for a week. The father told his daughter to back the trailer into the campsite. I couldn't believe it. The young girl backed in the trailer like a real professional. When she got out, she was smoking a small cigar. Then she unraveled and rolled out a small wire fence in front of the camper. When she opened the door of the camper, two ducks walked out of the trailer into a small area

A bear comes for a visit

where they stayed for the week. I can still smell the trailer after the ducks came out. I found out later that they were an advance team for a popular traveling circus. They went before the circus to put posters wherever they could. They turned out to be really good people. There were no problems during their stay. I talked to the father on many occasions about the circus. They were very interesting, but to say the least, they were very different. But this was not the end of the circus.

In the spring and fall we lived in Meriden during the week. However, if there was a need, I went down to the campsite during the week, too.

One fall, I was sitting at my desk at home in Meriden and got a phone call from a neighbor near the camp. He said, "There's a camper that just came in, and there's a bear in the campground." I wasn't surprised that a camper had simply come in. In those days, we had a kind of honor system. There was a mail chute at the entrance with registration cards and envelopes. A camper would register, put his money in the envelope and drop it in the mail chute. That was when cash was the order of the day since plastic hadn't come along yet.

Sometimes, though, people didn't pay. They just camped for free. I figured for the two or three dollars we lost, it wasn't worth having someone there in the off season. One day, although I never knew that someone used the campground, I received a letter from a woman in California. She wrote that they had been on the road traveling around the country and had stayed overnight. All they had was a big bill that was too much. They didn't have a checkbook with them. So, she wrote that they used the facilities and liked the campsite. She enclosed two or three dollars, whatever the rate was that night, and sent the money from California. That sort of thing restored my faith in human beings.

But, the bear incident was different. Usually, campers didn't bring bears along! "A bear?"

"Yeah, there's a B-E-A-R, bear! A big, brown bear chained to the tree!"

"You gotta be kidding me," I said into the phone.

"No," my friend said. "There's a group and they also have some kind of horse — a funny-looking horse, too."

"What the hell's going on?" I said.

"Yeah, you ought to come down here," my friend said.

Camper with the visiting bear

So, I took the kids, a couple of my kids' friends, called another friend, and said, "Come on, we're going down to the lake." It was fall. We flew down to the camp. Sure enough, there was what looked like Gentle Ben, the bear that was a big deal on the Gentle Ben show then, tied to a tree. A horse was tied to another tree, and a man was walking nearby with a monkey on a leash. I found out the unknown camper owned the bear and the monkey that were in the movie, *Kon Tiki*. (I never saw the movie). He let me take the monkey, and I walked down the road to my friend Paul Dunphy's campsite. I let the monkey climb on top of the Dunphy's family sign and snapped

The camping chimp

a photo of it to prove the monkey was there. The kids thought they were seeing a circus.

The kids got quite a kick out of the bear who was probably six feet tall. He was tame, so I got photos of him with the kids. The owner had clipped "Gentle Ben's" teeth and claws so he couldn't hurt anybody. Even though "Gentle Ben" bore his name well, I wouldn't let the kids get too near him. We erected a sign with the bear on it. The campsite number was on it to identify it. It is now in Campsite C, where Butch is today. Also, the monkey is on a sign on a tree that tells you what site it is.

The camper had a couple of other animals, although I can't remember what they were now. It turned out that he was entertaining some people in Hartford. The campers agreed it was quite a thrill to see him, though. It was the only bear I ever saw in the campground.

The fellow who owned the animals was evidently in some kind of a show or exhibit that the animals performed in. He gave us tickets to the show in another town and we attended the performance. It was quite a novelty.

I thought of starting a small zoo for the kids at the campground. One night a young fellow came up to me and said, "Mr. Gustine, do you want a fox?" For me, this was an unusual request, to say the least.

"Where in the heck are you going to get a fox?" I asked.

"I have a pet fox and I can get it for you," the boy said.

I thought he was pulling my leg. Another boy said that he saw a fox down at the beach one day. I couldn't believe this

Nelson Gustine and the camping bear

because foxes are usually pretty cautious animals. But, I had an animal cage. "Sure, I'll put it in a cage out in back of the old Quonset hut," I said. I told him to go get the fox, which he did.

The next day, the fox was in the cage. "Oh, my God," I said when

I saw the fox in the cage. The boy explained to me that the fox had become his pet — unheard of to me. But, one lives and learns, especially when there are kids around.

First animal in the zoo

I decided the fox would be the first animal in my zoo. Then I heard that foxes can contract fox fever as well as other diseases, and they can have rabies. I figured if a fox bit someone, it could become a serious legal problem for me. I called the veterinarian and told him about the fox. He said, "Having a pet fox is a sign that something's wrong. I can give the fox some shots so he won't turn out to be dangerous." I asked him how much the shots would cost. "About $200," he replied.

"I don't have $200," I said. That night, I went down to the cage, opened it, and let the fox go. That was the end of my zoo.

22

Hilary and Tom

Two men who worked for an electrical contractor came to our camp one summer. The married one, Hilary, had a wife and one son. The other one, Tom, was divorced. I just began to build the campground, and I told them they could camp down in the D Area. Hilary wanted to be in a remote area on top of the hill. I explained that there weren't facilities there — no electricity and no bathroom. At the time, I was building a couple of outhouses. He said, "Even though it's a rough road to get to it, if you give me the wood and let me go up there to camp, I'll build an outhouse in Area G." I said, "Well, that's okay." I gave him the wood and, sure enough, he built an outhouse and camped up there.

A few days later Hilary came to me and said, "Nelson, how about if I run electric wire up there so I can have electricity? I have enough wire to do that."

I said, "Well, that sounds okay to me." It was pretty hard to say no because he was helping me for free and seemed enthusiastic. So now he and his family were camping all by themselves up in what we today call G Area. With a bathroom and electricity, he was quite happy. I didn't know it at the time, but he and his family lost their rental, and he was looking for a place to live.

The next thing Hilary said to me was, "I have a small horse and I have a goat. Can you find me a place where I can put them while I'm camping?"

I said, "Well, you can put 'em over in that field," which I pointed to. There was nothing there at the time. That's what he did. Not too long after the horse and goat were in the pasture, a young girl went over there and started to feed apples to the horse. The horse turned around and bit her on the shoulder.

When I came home from work, I was told about it. The person said, "Hey, that horse bit a girl and her shoulder's all black-and-blue."

It certainly wasn't good news to me.

I went down to where the family was camping. The father was sitting very relaxed at the camp site. I asked to see the girl's shoulder. It looked bad. I said, "I'll bring her to the doctor to get her checked."

The father didn't seem overly concerned. He just said, "She'll be all right." But I didn't like that, so I asked for his permission to take his daughter to the doctor. He said, "Go ahead and take her." So I did. The doctor examined her and said to me that he couldn't find any break.

But she was really black-and-blue, and the spot was sore. The doctor said, "Well, I suggest we give her a tetanus shot just in case." That's what we did. Everything worked out all right. I was a little nervous because the bite was a really, really, gruesome sight. Her shoulder was totally black. When we got back, I moved the horse to another area which was a little safer and away from everybody. It worked all right for the rest of the season.

At the end of the season, Hilary told me that he found a rent for the winter, but he would be back in the spring. The following spring Hilary, his family, and Tom came back. I was very happy to see them because they did a lot of electric work for me last season, especially in A and B Areas.

My wife ran the store and a young girl helped her. I didn't pay much attention to Tom spending time with the helper. He was probably twice her age and was also a police officer. He drank quite heavily. I became nervous when I realized what Tom's character was like, and that he seemed to be spending so much time with her. One day Hilary said to me, "Nelson, you've helped me a lot with my family and camping and my animals. I know Tom pretty well. I can't sit back and watch Tom with this young girl. He's a fast mover, and when he drinks he's very dangerous. For sure as I'm standing here, that young girl's going to get in trouble with him. I've known him for quite a while, and I would suggest you do everything you can to break up that relationship."

Later I spoke to Tom. "She is a friend of mine," I began, "and I do not want you to spend time with her. She is much too young for you." About four days after talking to Tom, I was taking my walk around the camp at eleven thirty at night. I found them together down at the beach. He had obviously been drinking pretty heavily. I sent her back to her campsite and confronted him. The situation became quite tense because he was still drinking and it was hard to talk to him. I asked him to leave. When he didn't, I went back to the office and called the police. Two officers came in. Of course, Tom, being a policeman, knew them very well. He started to tell them his side of the story, which didn't make any sense to me. I just wanted him away because he was drinking. One of the officers seemed to take his side and tried to change the subject with me. I became a little impatient with the policeman and said, "I called you for a problem, and you're not helping the problem. You're adding to the problem, so I think you better leave." They did. That was the end of that night. Tom did go to bed after that incident.

The next day one of the officers, who didn't say much that night, came and apologized. He said, "I really don't know what happened last night."

I said, "Well, as far as I'm concerned I know you're an innocent party." Then he told me he wanted to come camping some time in the future. I said, "That's no problem, you can come any time you want." So that worked out pretty well. To my surprise, the next day Tom packed his bags and left. He didn't live too far away within the community, so he had a place to go. He was sober when he left, but he knew he wasn't wanted at the camp any longer. Thank God, that was the end of him.

Glenn, Bruce, and Mildred Gustine

Nelson and Mildred Gustine in 1984

Michele, Nelson, Mildred, and Glenn Gustine

Mini Golf

Bruce driving campground wagon ride

The pool

Carlene and Santa

Hazel and Ralph Gustine

Revolutionary War encampment

*Dolores Dunphy
and Mildred Gustine*

*Arts and Crafts
under the pavilion*

The crowd waiting for the peanut drop

Fourth of July

Dolores Dunphy, Mildred Gustine, and Dolly Lawrence

Nelson Gustine grading the land for the Quonset hut

View of Lake Pocotopaug from Nelson's Court

Hazel Gustine's 90th birthday

The honey wagon

Mildred Gustine at a Luau

The Fourth of July parade

The camp store

Hot air balloon

Clowning around

Nelson at an event

Monkey business

Sailing at the pond

Any excuse for a parade

Michele and Glenn Gustine

The campground in the fall

Bruce Gustine at Gustine's RV

23

Shady Guests

We had two houses for rent in Nelson's Court. A couple with two young girls rented the house in the front. Reggie, the father, was an ex-Navy man who served in the British Navy during World War II. With my experiences in World War II, we had a lot to talk about and became fast friends.

Sometime afterwards, Reggie met John. Reggie, his wife, and John became close friends. Although he did not stay in Reggie's house, John visited often. When John went to the local bars, he would always buy drinks for everyone, so he was known to everyone in town.

On one visit, John gave two brand new bicycles to Reggie's young girls. When my mother learned about this, she said, "Something's wrong. John doesn't meet the smell test." My mother could always tell someone's character no matter what — and often she was right!

Sometime later, when I was working in the yard, my mother came running out to me and said, "I told you. I told you."

"What are you talking about, Ma?"

"I just heard on the radio that two men were caught robbing a safe in a store in Middletown." Middletown, Connecticut was about half way between Meriden and East Hampton. For several weeks, the newspaper reported many break-ins.

Sure enough, one of the men was named John. We later found out he and his friend were in an Arkansas state prison for breaking into and robbing safes.

When Reggie and his wife heard this, they did not believe it was "their John," with whom they were such good friends.

But it was. John was sent to prison in Connecticut. Being loyal friends, Reggie and his wife visited him often. In fact, Reggie's wife put John on a pedestal because, to her, he was like Robin Hood — stealing from the rich and giving to the poor. Since they couldn't afford bicycles for their girls, they were grateful to John for them.

Sometime later, Reggie died. When John was released from prison, he and Reggie's wife started seeing each other. The relationship didn't last long. Perhaps John got cold feet. He took off for Arkansas, where he came from. We never heard from him again.

There are different kinds of shady characters. One summer a contractor came into the camp looking for a few campsites. His regular occupation was to remove asbestos in buildings. Because he couldn't find workers in our country to work for him, he hired young college kids from Ireland. All of them wanted to rent campsites from me for the duration of the contract. Their jobs paid well. The first thing the contractor did was buy a car at a used car lot. The understanding with the dealer was that they would be here for a month and a half and the dealer would then buy back the car.

After they were with us for a while, they located an Irish club about twenty miles away which they visited often to play pool and have a few drinks. Near the end of their work contract, they visited the club again. By now, there were only three of them at the club. It was during the period when a group of fighters was trying to fight the British in Ireland. That night, there were about thirty to forty people in the room listening to pro-Irish speakers. One of them was looking for donations to help fight the British. Another told a story about bad things that the British were doing, trying to elicit even more donations. One of the boys asked where and when the fighting happened. The speaker told him it happened two months ago in a particular village, whose name I have forgotten. The boy said, "That's my village and that never happened there. I was there." The situation at the club became quite tense. One of the speakers jumped off the stage and came toward the boy. Several of the people in the audience stood up and got between them. Two of the boys ran out of the building to get their car. They just bought groceries, so they wrapped a grocery bag around the license plate so no one could identify it. Then one of them drove the car to the front of the building and yelled to the third boy who ran out and dove into the car. They drove away towards Hartford, which was the opposite way home. They doubled back a couple of times to try to shake anybody who might be chasing after them.

At this point, they had three more working days to go on their contract. They decided they better get rid of the car so nobody could find them. The next day I drove them to the used car lot to return the car. With only a few more days to go they were very, very, nervous boys. They checked every single car that came and went, looking for a strange car. They were so nervous that they couldn't wait to go home. When their three days were up they flew home, and that was the end of that. I was very much surprised that nobody followed them back and that everything worked out, at least for me.

There was another shady guest. Someone in the campground found a pocketbook and turned it in to the lost and found department in the office. The office girl told me about it and said there was no name in it. I said I'd like to check it for myself. I looked in the pocketbook. I found two small mirrors, a razor blade, two small straws, and a small, empty plastic bag. I knew that these materials were used by some people on drugs. Now, I really wanted to know who owned the pocketbook, so I hung it on the wall so everyone could see it. I instructed the office girl to ask the person who claimed the pocketbook to sign a receipt, and find out what campsite the person was on. A day or so later, somebody came in and recognized her pocketbook. She was a fifteen-year-old girl who was staying with a seasonal camper and was on the site a week. The family she was camping with also had two young daughters about the same age. It didn't sound like a good idea to have her with them. Later that night I went to talk to the mother and father. I told them what I discovered without making a big deal out of it. They just could not thank me enough. They shook hands with me about four or five times and thanked me again and again. The father said, "We will take charge of this. She is leaving now." I never heard any more about her.

A young family camped with us for several years. The young boy was always trouble, never destructive but always involved with something. On many occasions I took him back to his father in the back of my truck. On one particular night when I brought him back to his father, the youngster started punching his father. A fistfight resulted. One of the next door neighbors, who was a little bigger than I, ran over. He grabbed the boy and threw him on the ground. This only encouraged more fighting. We had a no tolerance policy regarding physical fighting, so I said to the father, "Take your son home. Forget about camping for a while." I thought that was the end of it. But, eventually the family came back and the boy behaved. I guess he learned a lesson.

When I used to ride around the camp in my truck, there was always a young boy in the area who wanted to ride. One week a woman came to the office and said that someone stole stuff out of her camper. She said it had to be a small person to get through her screen door. The next day the boy was waiting for me to ride around the campground. He seemed to be the right size as the suspected thief. I spoke to him about somebody breaking into the camper's trailer. He told me that it was not him, "It was my brother." I was surprised by his admission. Then, I told the woman whose trailer was broken into that I found out who did it. She called the police. The woman also had words with the boys. By the time the police arrived at the scene, the family packed up and left. After they were gone, we checked around the campsite and found quite a few of the items that were stolen. It was truly obvious to me who did it.

Another thieving event occurred. One day I was in the big Rec. hall. A young boy came up to me and said, "That big boy at the pinball machine won't let anybody play the machine. He opens the door for the money and takes it out and keeps playing. He's been there quite a while." By the time the young boy got through telling me, the big boy left. I knew who he was.

Later that day I went to talk to the culprit's parents. When I got there the boy was sitting at the campsite with them. I told the parents I was there on business, not pleasure. I asked for permission to talk to the son. I also asked them not to interfere with what I was saying until I got all through. They agreed, not knowing what I was going to talk about. I looked straight at the boy and said, "You are a thief and you stole money out of my machine." Naturally, he denied it. I continued, "Someone told me he saw you do it. You stole several dollars out of the machine. Well, maybe it wasn't several dollars, it was probably $10 or $15."

For some unknown reason the boy said, "No, it wasn't $10, it was only $5." Both parents were very upset. I told the parents that I wanted their son to stay at the campsite and not roam around the campground alone any more.

A short time later the father came up to me and demanded to know who squealed on his son. I said, "The case is closed!" I could not believe the father asked that question. Later I found out the father went home, got his son's bicycle, drove his son out to the entrance of the camp, and gave him the bicycle so he could ride around downtown. I thought that was a very peculiar way to punish his son for theft.

The last straw with a thief was the one who stole Mil's last flower. With all the work that was done in establishing the camp, it didn't occur to us to do much landscaping for beauty, or even to plant flowers, for that matter. The area was even barren of wildflowers. Since Mildred loved flowers so much, one day I bought two tubs and planted flowers for her. The flowers flourished for most of the season. But then they began to die off so that, by the end of the season, only one red flower remained.

One day Mil and I were sitting out on our porch when a car came in driven by a young man. When he saw the flower, he stopped his car, jumped out, and stole the last flower. I ran out to my car and drove it as fast as I could and followed him. By this time, he arrived at his site where four or five people were sitting around a campfire, including his wife. He approached his site with Mil's red flower, making a big deal out of bringing it to his wife. When she saw him, she jumped up to receive the flower. I moved quite fast, so I was right behind him as he gave it to her. I took the flower out of his wife's hand and said to her in front of his friends, "Your husband stole Mil's last flower." Then I took the flower and left saying to myself, "Let him explain this situation to his wife."

As I've said, "There are all kinds of shady guests." Let me tell you another story that is true. The mobile home that we lived in was across the street from the big Rec. hall. One morning I woke up about six thirty to hear a commotion outside. I looked out the window and saw three police cars. It looked to me like the policemen were getting bulletproof jackets out of their trunk. I got dressed as fast as I could and went out. When I got to where I originally saw the police, they moved on to another area. I finally caught up with one of them in the

F Area. I told him who I was and asked, "What's going on?"

He said, "We're having trouble with propane here. We're waking everybody up and telling them to get out of the area because we don't want anybody to get hurt. I know you have a lot of campers moving around." Later, I found out why the police came. A woman and her boyfriend were in their camper. They worked at the atomic plant down in Haddam Neck. This particular morning, the girl shot a pistol in the camper. The boyfriend ran out and called the police. With his entry card, he let the police in. After the police got squared away with the girl, they told everybody to go back to bed. There was no danger of propane. They used that as an excuse to make sure everybody was out because they didn't know what was going to take place, and something dangerous could have happened. Luckily it didn't. After that incident, I wasn't very comfortable. Everybody was calling the woman "Pistol Pete." I decided the best thing to do was to see if I could find a way to get her to leave. At first, she was reluctant to go, but after a while she packed up and left.

The shadiest guest was a camper who stayed for a whole year. He said he hurt his leg and his back at work. He appeared to be very much in pain. Whenever he moved around he used a walker.

Once in a while he came to the store walking slowly. People realized he was in pain and felt sorry for him. At that time, at the end of the season, we always had a Halloween dance and everybody got dressed up. Some of the costumes were really quite original. One person in particular stood out. Usually I could figure out who everyone was even though they were in costume. But this one I couldn't figure out. He was all covered up and dancing the jig with somebody else having a great old time. All of a sudden, he turned around, gave me a bear hug and he said, "Nelson." When he said my name, I recognized the voice. He was jumping around having a great old time with no walker in sight. He realized that I recognized him. He never came back to the Rec. hall again. He stayed on the grounds for a while, but never came near me. I heard he went to Florida and he was applying for aid. He already appealed and was trying to get a ruling from Workers' Comp. on his total disability. I knew he was nothing but a fraud, a real shady character.

24

Potluck Dinners

In the beginning of camping at Nelson's, we had a potluck supper under the pavilion. Everybody brought a dish. It looked like it was going be a lot of fun. We told people to bring their own dishes to hold whatever they wanted to eat from the buffet. The problem was that many people brought trays instead of dishes and piled their

Campers enjoy a potluck dinner

trays with food. The two staff people and I noticed what was going on and realized that there was not enough food for everyone. In fact, near the end of the potluck supper there were only two carrots left! Somebody brought them up to me and said, "This is all there is left, so I guess you guys can have carrots." I was hungry so I bought pizzas for Mil, our friends, and me. Perhaps people thought there would no longer be potluck suppers.

However, I can always find something positive in everything that happens. I decided to change things around. I was talking to my friends about it looking for ideas. One person said to me, "All you need are volunteer servers to serve the food." That sounded like a great idea to me, so that's what we did. I always asked for fellow volunteer servers. I usually had no problem finding volunteers. I always told the servers to give everybody the same amount of food. "And remember, you're the last ones to eat," I cautioned them. "Nobody gets seconds until everybody's had at least one serving."

Once we had the big Rec. hall up and running, we decided to hold two potluck suppers a season, one in the spring and the other in the fall. The idea of the spring supper was for everybody to introduce themselves to get to know who their neighbors were. But, it was difficult to get everybody together in the spring because some people weren't camping yet and were timid. We stopped having the spring potluck. The fall one was popular for a long, long time. However, I guess the novelty wore off on that also because it became difficult to get enough people to make it worthwhile, so we stopped having those too.

25

Building the Rec. Hall

Unloading steel for the Rec. hall

As the campground kept getting bigger and more and more campers came, it was obvious that we needed a larger building. I started to do some research. There was a campground in Massachusetts called "Robbin's Farm." I visited it before to see what it was like. I remembered he had a large building there.

One day, Mildred, my father-in-law, and I took a ride up to Robbin's Farm to look at his building. It was constructed of wood and looked pretty nice. We agreed that it was pretty neat and would fit into the theme of what we were trying to do.

Since I am not one to jump into anything, I needed to find another building to compare it to before deciding to build one like it. While I continued my research, we had a tremendous snowfall that caused the Civic Center roof in Hartford to collapse from the weight of the snow. I didn't think too much of it myself. However, a camper who had a friend that camped at Robbin's Farm saw me with a salesman. He said, "Nelson, just for your information, the building that this fellow built up in Robbin's Farm collapsed from the snowstorm with a bunch of trailers inside it in storage."

When the salesman came back with an estimate, I said to him, "Hey, by the way, I understand your building fell down."

"Yes, it did," he said. "We found something that wasn't right, but we reengineered it and corrected all that."

I was leery though about hiring him. So, I visited other campgrounds and found a building made of metal that I liked even better in a campground in New Jersey. We visited it several times.

Eventually, I contacted the supplier of the metal and began asking him questions. He said, "You have good questions, and I have the answers. You can ask me all the questions you want to."

Footings for the Rec. hall

One day, the metal supplier called me right out of the blue. He said, "Nelson, the price of steel is going to be affected in a month and it will go up ten percent." It was a time when prices were going crazy. He continued, "I have the steel in the yard that you need right now. I know you're serious about what you're doing because your questions are so intelligent. So, if you want to buy the steel now, I'll sell it to you at the current price. It would be better to have than money in the bank because the price is only going to go up!"

I told him I'd get back to him. Then, I thought about what he said. I said to myself, "You know, Nelson, you should just buy the darn steel." It was about $5,500. Where I was working, lots of trucks were coming and going all the time. To one of the drivers, I said, "Do you ever come back deadhead?" In other words, with an empty truck.

"Yes, all the time," he said.

"How would you like to do me a favor?" I asked him.

"Sure," he said.

"How about stopping and picking up that steel for me and bringing it to my campground? Of course, I'll pay for the cost of the gas."

"Yes, on one condition, though," he said. "I'll bring it to you on Saturday because I have to have the trailer truck on the road Monday morning. Who will help me unload it?"

"No problem," I said. "We'll get it off, don't worry." I had the backhoe at that time, so I picked it up off the truck and made a big pile of steel on the building site.

My idea was to buy the steel and leave it there until we got around to building. However, once the steel was there, I kept looking at it.

A picnic in the Rec. hall

The wheels in my head started turning trying to figure out how we would get the building up.

The first thing we had to do was dig foundations for the steel. I contacted my friend, George Hall. He was a good motivator. He gathered all the young boys together and said to them, "We're going to build a bunch of sandboxes and I need you guys to help." He got the kids up there digging all these holes. They didn't know why they were digging, except that they would have a lot of sandboxes to play in, they thought. In fact, one of those kids who is all grown up reminded me about it not too long ago. "He had us all fooled right to the very end. We were working like crazy," said Bobby Robinson, "and we thought we were going to build a bunch of sandboxes." Anyway, that's how we got our footings built for the new building.

George Hall and his wife were avid square dancers. He tried to get me to put a second floor on the Rec. hall for square dancing. At the time, I didn't feel that I could afford more expenses. I ended up building one floor. Today, when I look back and think, it probably was the right decision.

*Nelson and Mildred work
on the Rec. hall*

Next, I applied for a building permit. The building inspector not only issued a permit to build, but he also wanted to help lay it out.

My father-in-law was a machinist who was capable of drawing up the plans on paper and then explaining how it would all be done. He said, "We're going to pour these concrete circles like for a foundation. You have to put bolts in there so the steel sits right on the bolts. Once you get it on the bolts, if they don't tie in up on top, we're in trouble. So, everything has to be on the money."

We realized that we couldn't do the actual steel work, so we found a sign company in Meriden, Connecticut, that knew how to work with steel. The owner said his company could put up the building. I made a deal with him, and gave him the plans that my father-in-law had drawn up. He and his men brought a crane, and like a jigsaw puzzle, put it all together. My sons and their friends, who were between eight and eleven years old, watched the whole show.

When the crew went to lunch, they left all their gear out. The kids went back to get their own gear. They put on their helmets and belts and it looked like they were going to finish the job. They were playing near the steel beams.

Word travels fast when construction is going on. Others came

Nelson's Rec. hall work crew

on their own lunch hours to see what was happening. One of them said to me, "You do everything on a shoestring. How'd you get that building up?"

I said, "Oh, I got my own crew. That's how we got it up." They all looked at the kids in disbelief, but how could they argue? The kids looked like they were doing the work.

When the beams were ready to go up, it was going to be a delicate operation. Each one was 2x12 and twenty feet long. We put two trucks in there and two ladders, took one beam at a time, and kept pushing each one up very slowly. It was dangerous because once you had it up, there wasn't much room to move.

As luck would have it, and I was often lucky, one of the Frenchmen that was at the camp for a long time came by with his gang. "When are you going home for dinner, Nelson?" he said.

"I'm about ready right now."

"Do you mind if we put some

The Rec. hall roof

The Rec. hall which had the office, a store, and an open area for activities

of those beams up for you?"

"Oh," I answered, "be my guest." By the time, we got back from dinner, they had put up about twenty beams. They seemed to be throwing them around like they were made of cardboard. It was unbelievable. So, between them and our crew, we managed to get them all up, which was a blessing because they were really heavy.

The next job was getting the plywood on to make the roof. Once we did that, the building could be used, although it wasn't fully closed in. We had music in there with a DJ named Chuck Skoog. People came with their babies and laid the blankets on the dirt floor and danced. It was pretty dusty at times, but we all had a lot of fun.

The next year, we decided to close it all in. I had to buy wood to do so. Two young Frenchmen who camped at Nelson's were in the sheetrock business. One of them lived in Colchester. His wife was pregnant. They liked our son, Glenn, so she named her baby Glenn, which I thought was pretty neat.

Mil and I were about to leave for a campground owner's convention in Florida. The Frenchmen asked if they could stay later in the season while we were away. I gave them a key to lock the gate when they left. I said to them, "If you would like to put up some of the siding for us, be my guests."

When we got back, the siding was three-quarters of the way up the building. They did it in one weekend, and I wasn't even there. It was unbelievable.

The next thing we did was lay a concrete floor. We had to be sure that it wouldn't freeze and crack on us. We hurried to close the Rec. hall in and get it squared away before winter. With the sides on, even without the heat, it wouldn't be as bad as being out in the open where the floor would surely crack in the cold. So that's what we did. That's why there aren't any cracks in the floor.

The only problem with a concrete floor is keeping it clean. It seems that there is a solution for everything, though. We always charged visitors who weren't campers a fee to visit the camp. It used to be $2.00.

Dedication plaque in the Rec. hall for Fred Kaiser

A smart, young lad met a girl in the campground and he always wanted to visit with her. He couldn't afford the $2.00 each time. One day he said, "Mr. Gustine, I'm a helper at a tile company. We lay tiles on floors. We get a lot of jobs sometimes with a lot of tile left over, and they're nice tiles, but we can't do anything with the extras." I had an idea what was coming. He said, "I'll make you a deal. I'll tile the store floor for you in the Rec. hall if you give me a season pass to come and go and not stop."

I said, "You're sure about that?"

He said, "Yeah, no problem. You can even call my boss. In fact, if you like, I'll have my boss call you." The boss called me to verify the lad's idea.

I said, "That's great. We clean the floor up and you put your tiles on, and I'll punch you a ticket and you can come and go as you please." The two young people were really happy about the lad's "job." It was great for me because we had a nice tile floor that was easy to take care of.

Not long after the Rec. hall was completed, two girls came along from Canada on bicycles. They were on their way to Florida. They graduated high school and had some college. They were very, very, attractive, so they caught everyone's eye. The weather wasn't very warm. They had pup tents to sleep in. This meant that they'd be sleeping along the side of the road. It made me uncomfortable to think of them being out in the open. I said to them, "The best thing for you girls is to sleep in the Rec. hall." They were grateful.

The next day, I had to go back to Bristol to work. I offered to take them and their bicycles in my station wagon to Route I-84 to get them started toward Florida. I said, "Remember, it's illegal to ride a bicycle on a state highway in most places. So, if the police stop you — and don't stop for anyone else — speak Canadian French. Then they won't know what you're talking about." They laughed, but understood.

"Also," I said, "I'm concerned about you. You gotta be careful where you park along the way. I want you to promise me that you will drop me a card from Florida to tell me you got there okay."

About a week or two later, I received a card that read, "We arrived. Thanks."

26

Entertaining the Kids

Someone suggested I do something for the kids, especially since kids seemed to get into trouble if they weren't occupied. One idea was to open a bale of hay up in the field, throw coins into it, and then let the kids scramble for the coins. Everything we did in the beginning was a learning experience.

To begin, we lined all the kids up at the store. Then I gave the signal to go. They all charged and tore through the hay trying to find coins. The mistake we made was we didn't separate the kids by age or size. When the bigger ones ran, they scrambled into the smaller ones. I thought they'd kill them! We couldn't stop the momentum.

Searching for coins in the hay

Luckily, no one was hurt. Going forward we usually divided the kids into three groups by age and size, and each group went at a different time. That way, everybody had a fair chance. The big ones couldn't bully the smaller ones. Everyone seemed happy with the arrangement.

I thought another suggestion that came up was good. One night I purchased six watermelons and hid them in the campground around the area of the new big Rec. hall. The next day I told the kids a dinosaur came the night before into the campground and laid some big eggs. This story created excitement among the younger kids. I told them that we were going out to see if we could find the eggs. I also said the eggs looked and tasted like watermelon. "If you find one," I said, "bring it back to the Rec. hall and we'll have a piece of the eggs." So, I said, "Let's go, kids." The kids ran out of the Rec. hall fast, as fast as jackrabbits. A short time later five watermelons were found and brought back. They could not find the sixth one. I knew where I planted it, so went out to check myself, but I couldn't find it either. It was a mystery to me.

Later on, however, I learned that two big kids who were unaware of what we were doing, were walking around. They found the big watermelon and, of course, picked it up and took it to their campsite. By the time we discovered it, they were sitting at the campsite with other kids eating the watermelon. It was a good learning situation. Everybody had fun.

27

Entertaining the Adults

We had a Dress Up Contest where the men dressed as women. Ten or fifteen men waited outside the rear side door to make an entrance. Of course, men being men, they were clowning around with each other. An actual woman tried to enter the building where the men were waiting. She found herself in the middle of all these

Winner of the Dress Up Contest

men dressed as women. Not knowing that she was a real woman, the guys included her in their fooling around. Then they discovered she was a woman. They started to yell to each other to knock it off because there was a real woman in the crowd. She was a good sport and laughed it off. The Rec. hall was standing room only.

The next year we had control of where the people entered. We also made a sign to prevent the same thing from happening again, which could have ended up being a serious problem.

We provided another form of adult entertainment. One day as I went to work, I looked up in the sky and there was a hot air balloon. That set my wheels in motion. I soon found out who owned the balloon and made a deal with them to come to the campground. The deal was I would furnish the gas propane and he would charge people for a ride and keep the money. That was a good deal for me because it gave my campers something exciting to do. In fact, it was a good deal for both of us. He got to make some money.

When he arrived with the balloon, he tied the balloon to a truck with a sturdy rope. Then he took people for rides. They went up in the air and then come down. It was quite sensational to watch the balloon suspended over the campground. He and the balloon campers looked happy. The next morning he took six people for a longer actual ride over the camp and over the lake. It was an interesting ride. At the end of the ride he landed in a farmer's yard on the other side of the lake. He was happy with the number of campers who took the ride. I think he charged $50 each for the ride. We wanted to do it again, but that was the only time we did it because he left after the ride and never came back.

We often provided musical entertainment. I met a country western band, and hired them to come and play at our campground. The people gathered around to listen to the hillbilly music, and they appeared to enjoy the band. Everything seemed to be going great. Then the complaints started. A woman said, "Nelson, you're trying to run a family campground, but that fellow's telling jokes that are not very

Musical entertainment

family-oriented." I didn't go to listen this particular time because I had other work to do.

I said, "I don't like the sound of that either." So, I went down to listen the next time they played. Sure enough, after it was over I told the leader, "This is a family campground and your adult jokes are not permitted in this camp-

ground." I figured that would stop the jokes because I booked them for several more engagements, and I assumed they wanted to continue playing. However, some time later, somebody said, "Hey, that guy's telling the same jokes again."

I said, "You have to be kidding me." So, I went down. He was telling the same dirty jokes. This time, I fired the band. I felt badly for my campers because they liked the music, and they could have continued entertaining us. But, I couldn't approve of entertainment that could corrupt the children.

Most people like to go to weddings and our campers were no exception. Several people got married in the camp. For one couple in particular it was a second marriage, so marriage wasn't new to them. However, Mil and a few other women decided to make it a memorable event. They decorated an area for the wedding with beautiful decorations. One female camper was a Justice of the Peace, so she married the couple. After the wedding all the campers in the area had a big party for them. It was a great big event.

A camper's wedding

On Saturday nights, we had a game night with prizes for the winners. Since dice and wheels were illegal, and we didn't want to break the law, we devised a game where we placed cards with numbers on the wall. Contestants threw darts to hit the numbers. If they missed, there were beanbags on the floor, which were also numbered. If a guest hit a number on the wall or on the beanbag, he or she got a prize.

One thing I always wanted was an Indian powwow as entertainment. We managed to make a contact with a person who was involved with it. He told me that his group would come in and stage one. He also said that the idea of a powwow can entertain for about four or five years and then the novelty wears off. We held the powwows yearly. Sure enough, four years later it died down. People were no longer interested, so we stopped having them.

Teepee in the spillway

28

The Horseshoe Pits

Some of the men were looking for something to do. They came to me with the idea of building some horseshoe pits. In B Area, next to the playground, there was room for two pits. I told them I would get the wood, but they had to build them. They agreed and it worked out great. The only problem was it was near the camping area in B. The horseshoe pits were very successful. The men really enjoyed them.

I lived down the street from the campground. One Sunday morning I came early to the camp. Four women were waiting for me at the office. They camped in B Area and were pretty irate and very upset. The night before, when it was dark, the men drove their cars down to the horseshoe pits and left their headlights on so they could play after dark. The women said they were tired enough of listening to the horseshoes banging and banging during the day. Now they had to listen to them when it was dark, and that was the last straw. I told them to be patient while I looked for another location for the pits. I did, and today we have four horseshoe pits far enough away from the campsites. There are plenty of horseshoe pits which are used every single weekend. We even installed lights so the men can play at night and not disturb anyone.

Once the pits were built, the next thing the horseshoe players asked for was a bathroom building. I had an extra chemical toilet so we put it up there.

There was always a crowd, especially on Saturday and Sunday mornings to play horseshoes. It was a great thing to do that wasn't very costly.

At one time, groups of people challenged other campgrounds. They went and others came to play. Our campers won a couple of trophies which, today, hang up in the Rec. hall. So, putting the toilet near the horseshoe pits was worthwhile. It wasn't expensive and we probably get more use out of that than anything else.

29

Christmas in August

We were always looking for new and entertaining ideas to keep our guests occupied. Every year, we had a Christmas in August weekend. It seemed that every guest had an idea how to celebrate. Mildred and I discussed all of them and talked to different people about them. One guest worked in an airport and told us his good friend had an airplane. He said to me, "Why don't you hire my friend to fly over the campground and drop peanuts?"

Christmas in August with the Gustine family

After I overcame my hysteria at this preposterous idea, I thought about it. It was a fantastic idea, I decided. However, peanuts were not a Connecticut-grown food, and not as popular as they are today. As I said, you meet all kinds of people, and word travels fast in a campground. When one of our campers heard we needed peanuts, he said to me, "My friend is going to Pennsylvania where she says there are plenty of peanuts. She would be happy to bring some back to you."

First prize Best Decorated Campsite

The idea was taking root. She brought back the peanuts. I hired the pilot to fly his plane over the campground as we played Christmas music for everyone to hear. It was really exciting having Christmas in August. In fact, I got goose bumps in all my excitement.

All the campers assembled in the big field, a hay field, as the plane flew over to drop the peanuts. Wind was blowing strongly, so

Santa visiting during
Christmas in August

when he opened the plane's door, the bags flew out! But, they didn't land in the field. They landed in a nearby neighbor's yard. It seemed like everyone at once yelled, "Wow!" It was kind of disappointing.

A woman came over to us and said, "Don't you think you could have planned this a little better?"

Meanwhile, everyone was complaining to the pilot who was flying the old World War II plane. Someone said, "No wonder it took us so long to get rid of the Germans during World War II. You can't even drop your bags of peanuts in the right place."

There is always the killjoy. One of the guests said, "This is a great experiment. Do you realize that you could be arrested for throwing things out of an airplane?"

"Oh, really?"

"Yes," the guest continued. "You could hit somebody. Technically, a bag of peanuts could break on someone's head."

I realized that the first time a bag fell on someone's head or in someone's yard, I'd lose some control over the situation, and I didn't want that!

When the next August came, I figured I was going to get it right. The night before our planned Christmas in August, I drove to the hayfield and scattered peanuts all over.

The next day we played Christmas music, and everyone lined up near the field. I yelled to the crowd. "You can't go on the hayfield yet because he's going to drop peanuts and they might hit you." I sported a walkie-talkie, and pretended to be talking to the pilot. The crowd didn't know it was a fake because it was so noisy.

As the plane flew over the field, I kept saying, "There it goes. There it goes. The bags are broken and the peanuts are coming down. Let's go, let's go." It's hard to see a single peanut fly through the air, so the crowd just followed me.

I painted some of the peanuts red. If a guest found a red one, it was worth $5.00. A man came over to me afterwards and said, "My daughter found a red peanut and she ate the whole darn thing, painted shell and all."

Mildred decorating the top of the Christmas Tree

I said, "She ate $5.00."

"Yes," he said, "but, my question to you is, what kind of paint did you use on the peanuts?"

"Well, we use paint that we use in our arts and crafts activities. Don't worry, it's not lead paint."

"Good. That's all I wanted to know. So, it's okay that she ate the shell."

I think I got off easy. He didn't get $5.00. I used it for something else.

We decided we better not have this activity again, although we continued to have our yearly Christmas in August.

We found another thing to do in August. One weekend my wife and I went to a convention for campground owners in Massachusetts. One of the speakers talked about the joy she had getting her campground running at the beginning of the season and how she looked forward to the headlight parade. Everyone could relate to that. She continued to speak about the challenges of running the campground and how tired she got when it was near the end of the season. She said at the end of August she began to look forward to the taillight parade. Mildred never forgot that. At the end of every season from then on she would remind me about getting ready for the taillight parade. So, we also instituted a parade at the end of our season, and everyone enjoyed it.

30

Battle of Mott Hill

Troops line up before the battle

One of the big events at the camp was the "Battle of Mott Hill." One of the longest-time campers, Butch, was with us for forty-two years. He was passionate about the Civil War. Since I always loved learning about the Civil War, I soon found out there were quite a few campers who showed the same interest. We got together and put on a display of many different items of Civil War memorabilia.

Several campers collected uniforms, mostly from the North. So we decided to reenact the war. About fifteen or sixteen "volunteers" donned their uniforms. The women wore dresses of the period.

All the men had rifles and one man, Cookie, had a Civil War cannon that he brought down for the battle. All the men formed two lines, one for the South and one for the North. They started shooting blanks like they were shooting at each other. It created quite a commotion for the onlookers.

Cookie had a son who was about ten years old. It appeared that he was shot. After the battle two soldiers carried Cookie's son out of the battle area to where I was. He looked pretty bad to me. Later on, I said, "You had me fooled. My heart was in my mouth. For a few minutes I thought he got hurt for sure." All the men said the joke was on me because they saw I was really taken in by it all.

After the battle everyone enjoyed a beer. But, we had a rule that no one could drink alcohol until all the guns were put away. That worked out well, so we never had a problem.

Vendors

Women of the encampment

Cannon demonstration

Members of the encampment

Mildred Gustine

31

Fun Times

Campers announce the Bubblegum Hunt

Campers participate in the Bubblegum Hunt while a goat looks on

On Sundays, checkout time was three o'clock. Earlier in the afternoon, I would scatter pieces of bubblegum in wrappers all over the field. At two o'clock, we would ring the bell for the children to line up on one side of the field. After they got there, I let them go to find the gum. It was my treat and it kept them busy until checkout.

One day a family was trying to leave the camp early. The bubblegum hunt wasn't beginning for another fifteen minutes. I heard a commotion and went to investigate. A father was trying to get both of his daughters into the car so he could leave. The daughters were pretty adamant about staying for the hunt. He got one into the car, and then the other got out. To make people happy, I offered to give the girls some bubblegum, but they didn't want it. Then I said, "I'll throw a couple of pieces into the field so you can go get them." They didn't want that. They wanted to be in the hunt with all the other children. Finally the father raised his hands up as if to say, "What are you going to do?" He tried to get me to do the bubblegum hunt early. But I couldn't. It was called for two o'clock so I had to honor that. The daughters were quite thrilled! They didn't even care if they found bubblegum or not. They just wanted to be in the hunt.

A camper gave me a large bell, which he mounted as high as he could at the end of the Rec. hall. He attached a rope to the ringer so

Fourth of July parade
with children

Children in the
Halloween parade

we could grab it to ring the bell. Everybody knew when they heard the bell ringing that an activity was ready to begin. People swarmed to the Rec. hall so they wouldn't miss anything.

Parades are always fun, so we had them on Memorial Day, the Fourth of July, and other times. The children carried pots and pans and hit them with sticks to make "music" as they marched around the campground. Sometimes, we even had dog parades where everybody who had a dog would bring it. We had a contest to determine which one was the prettiest dog, or which one did the best trick, etc. These parades and contests were usually on a Saturday.

People wanted something more for entertainment than just sitting around the campfire. Often, we had music. On several occasions we hired a hypnotist or a magician to entertain the people, which everyone seemed to like. Campers had a lot of fun.

Another thing that created a little excitement for the adults was "betting" on saltwater crabs. I went down to the shore to buy them. When the bell rang, campers made a big circle in the Rec. hall. I put numbers on the crabs and placed them in a bucket which I turned upside down. Once everyone was in place, I'd lift the con-

Crab races in 1996

tainer and let the crabs out. The person who picked the number on the first crab across the line won. It was very exciting.

We had another popular event on Labor Day. During the weekend, campers took chances on what we called the "Wheel of Chance." The "wheel" was a large circle on a piece of cardboard. Sections were marked off and campers signed their names on a section. Just before checkout time on Labor Day, we hung the "wheel" up in the Rec. hall. Everyone came down to hopefully collect a prize. Once everyone was there, one of the campers threw a dart at the "wheel." On whatever name it landed, that person would be the winner.

Bird lady

Judo demonstration

Pie eating contest

Pet parade

***Mildred Gustine
running an activity***

***Children scramble in the
Bubblegum Hunt***

32

Fireworks

Most of the water pipes in the early days were just laid on top of the ground because we weren't open in winter. When the season ended, we drained the water so they wouldn't freeze. In D Area, the pipes in sites 6, 7, and 8 were buried about four to five inches underground primarily so that someone wouldn't trip on one. Fireplaces were placed about ten to fifteen feet away from water pipes. One rule for the entire camp was not to move any fireplace.

A group of three camping families needed three sites, so they moved one of the fireplaces to a more convenient spot for them and their tents. One morning they placed a fireplace on top of the one-inch plastic pipe under fifty pounds of pressure. Saturday night, about nine thirty, with all three families sitting around the fireplace, the heat finally was enough to melt the one-inch plastic pipe. I was not at the camp at the time, but later was told that the screams could be heard all over the campground. The water carried the fire up and over everyone including the tents. Luckily, the water continued and put out the fire. Nobody was hurt, and no equipment was damaged. Even today I think that those campers probably remember this experience and will for the rest of their lives. That was the only time we had such an event happen to us.

Although in the beginning we permitted fireworks on the property, it didn't last very long. We told the campers they could go down to the pond to shoot fireworks if they wanted to. Most of them went down to the pond with sparklers. However, one morning after some fireworks went off the night before, a camp worker came to me and said, "You'd better go down to the pond area because that's where we were working, and the place is littered with metal pieces from the sparklers and paper from the fireworks. It's really a mess."

That same year, a kid was sitting in Area E where there was a big campsite. He had a firework, but didn't realize that it was a rocket. He lit it and it flew across two campsites right into a window of one of the campers. Thank God someone was there to put out the fire. It could have burned the trailer down if no one saw it. It scared the heck out of the campers.

We decided not to allow fireworks after that because they could be quite dangerous. People wouldn't clean up after themselves. There were also too many people who didn't seem to understand the seriousness of clowning around with fireworks. We told anyone caught shooting fireworks to pack their bags and leave. We've continued this policy right up until today.

33

Don't Fool with Nature

Problems with nature can occur at any time, and they often happen in campgrounds.

We were always very fussy about people cutting down our trees. Some campers brought hammers and saws, picked the tree they wanted, and took an axe to chop it down. To us this was a big no-no. One day a man was down in the B Area where we already cut down a lot of trees. One tree left on the site wasn't in good shape and was quite high. We didn't have the equipment to reach it. He asked if he could have the tree. I gave him permission to cut it down. He couldn't do it right away, which was okay with me.

Millie and I lived down the street. We received a phone call one dark night from a neighbor who said that somebody was cutting trees in the campground and when a tree fell, it made quite a racket. I immediately jumped in my car and flew up to the site, forgetting that I gave the man permission to cut the tree. When I reached the area, it was him. By the time I arrived, the job was done. I said to the tree chopper, "What's the matter with you? Why would you do this at night and wake the town up?"

"Well, you told me I could chop it down."

"Yes," I said, "that's true, but you don't do something like this in the middle of the night. You scared me and the people around here half to death."

Another time I got a call that a woman was cutting the bark off my birch tree. Again, I flew to the area and saw that sure enough, she stripped the bark off. She made a fire in a nearby fireplace and was cooking the bark to make birch tea, so she said. She denied that she stripped the tree even though she had the bark in the pot. It was unbelievable to me that she lied to my face. It took a lot of moxie on her part to do this. I said, "Birch trees are usually valued at from $150 to $300. I estimate this one to have a value of $150, so I'm going to report you to the police for theft." I really had no intentions of doing so, but I wanted to scare her. I left.

When I returned, she had put out the fire, packed her bags and left. Obviously, she didn't want to get caught and have to pay a fine for stealing tree bark.

Rain causes many problems, too. When I arrived at the camp one Friday, I saw that three campers set their tent up in an area opposite C Area on a campsite where the water usually ran through it when we had a big storm. I went to see them. They were hooked up to the electricity, had their tent ready, and were all set to go to bed. I told them what would happen, but they refused to move saying it probably wouldn't rain. They thought everything would be okay and wanted to stay there. So I said, "Well, you're the bosses." The next night, at one thirty in the morning, I was home sleeping and woke up to a thunderstorm. Rain was coming down in torrents. When I went up to their site at nine thirty Sunday morning, they left their soaking wet mattresses, which were sitting on the ground, right where the water came through. They didn't drown, but I guess they'll never forget that experience.

A nice brook runs through the center of the campground that is fairly calm, but one particular time, a woman from New York City came and wanted to camp in the woods. When she saw the brook, she thought it was so beautiful that she decided to camp right there. It was okay because there wasn't too much water in the brook. However, that night, there was a tremendous downpour and thunder, so the brook rose rapidly. It made a lot of noise in the process. She was supposed to stay two or three days. However, the next afternoon, she came to Mildred and said, "You'll have to find me another campsite because I can't stand camping down near that brook. The water's running, and I can hear it. When I hear the water, it makes me want to go to the bathroom. I had to get up a half-dozen times last night to go to the bathroom because of that damn brook!"

Mildred suggested she move about one hundred feet away. The woman did and she was content there — for a while. However, the next morning, she came back up to Mildred and said, "Oh, you've got to find me a place out in the open. I can't stand it."

"What's the matter?" Mildred asked.

"There's a crow's nest in the top of the tree, and there are crows that are yapping all night. I can't stand it. I've got to get out of there."

Mildred told me about it. I knew there were crows, but we never paid much attention to them. I went to the camper and said, "New York City has all those noisy trains and buses. In the country, you hear the beautiful sounds of nature, like the music of the water running in the brook and the birds singing in the trees. I guess you better go out in the middle of the field to have a little peace and comfort away from all this country noise."

So, that's what she did. She was quite humorous about the whole thing. She stayed the whole time she intended. Every day is a new experience here for me.

Electricity has been known to create havoc. We installed a pay telephone at the pavilion in case anyone wanted to make a call. During storms, people sometimes sought shelter there. One day, a violent thunderstorm was raging. Two school teachers were camping with us at the time. One of the teachers was using the phone during the storm. A camper told me a teacher was hit by electricity, flew up in the air, and fell down. She was not seriously hurt, but she was surely shaken up.

I called the phone company and told them what happened. They came immediately and checked out the phone. In those days, phones were rented by the month from the phone companies, not owned as they are today. Nothing was found to be wrong with the phone, but the telephone company worker drilled four more ground rods into the ground that would keep a person from getting shocked again. We never had any problems after that.

34

Good Ideas, but Not Good Enough

A professor from UConn who came to the camp was quite a guy. He knew a lot about camping. He gave me a lot of ideas about camping before I was too involved. I invited his wife and him to see the property. He recommended that I build a tower on top of the woods that is now G Area. He thought campers would like to hike up to the tower to look down to see beautiful Lake Pocotopaug. In the fall when the leaves were off the trees, I went up there myself and climbed about ten feet up a tree. Sure enough, it was a beautiful spot.

Later, when I was in a local restaurant, a helicopter landed in the parking lot. Bells rang in my head, so I asked the pilot what he would charge to carry four telephone poles up to the top of the hill and drop them in holes that I would dig beforehand. He said, since he came from Pennsylvania, it would be $1,500 an hour. I decided not to go ahead because it was much too costly. I still think it might have been a good idea.

Another camper was interested in building a par three golf course. I didn't even know what that was at the time. He spent three or four days roaming around the land and measuring with his tape measure. Then he did some math. Finally, he told me that a par three golf course would work. I was not a golfer so I was not too enthused.

I thought it would be a good idea to put floats out in the middle of the pond making them into a golf hole. Campers could golf trying to hit balls into the ring on the other side of the pond. I bought some golf balls that were supposed to be floating golf balls. But when I tried them, they sank. They didn't float! We did retrieve some golf balls, which I still have.

Another idea that was run by me was to have a water slide way up on top of G Area that would end in the pond. That sounded like a pretty novel idea, but I wasn't so happy about that because it was dangerous.

One idea that had a little merit to it was to build a track for electric car races. Another campground was quite successful with a track. However, we didn't have anyone to manage it full-time.

Another idea that the guys were very interested in was to build a horseshoe pit indoors. We already had one outdoors. Some of the places did that quite successfully. But the problem was that the only time it would be workable would be in the winter. I wasn't about to heat my Rec. hall at that time. We'd also have to plow the snow and I didn't have equipment for that.

How about building a roller skating rink in the Rec. hall? I was asked. I used to love roller skating. The idea fascinated me, but then I realized the hall really wasn't big enough. We have a lot of tables and chairs in it. Everything would have to be taken out, or it could be dangerous, so we didn't do it.

Gardening is always a popular idea. A seasonal camper said he was looking for something to do. "How about if I find an area where we can plant a garden, like a structured garden so that everybody can participate in it if they wanted to?" he asked us. We thought it was a fine idea, but I was building a campground. I didn't have time to build a garden area even if he ended up finding a halfway decent spot where we could put it. I said to him, "What would happen if you put it together and the next thing you know you have to leave the campground?" That was the end of that idea.

Another idea was that since we had a pavilion and a store, how about having a Thanksgiving weekend? I said, "Thanksgiving was always a family day." A camper insisted that several campgrounds in Massachusetts were so crowded that weekend that you couldn't even get in there because so many people came. I still didn't see how we could do it. He said, "We'll close off part of the pavilion and put in portable heat. We'll take care of all that," he continued. "We'll supply a potluck-type Thanksgiving dinner." It sounded good, but it was a November thing and we close the camp for the season by then.

He was persistent, so suggested I go to another campground for Thanksgiving. I called for reservations. They were all filled up for that year, and I didn't want to obligate my family for the next year.

In the Rocky Hill area of Connecticut are dinosaur tracks. The state built a dinosaur park there. My thinking was to have a dinosaur exhibit just for campers. They could see it and would be steered to go to the dinosaur park. I was trying to figure out where I could get something that resembled a dinosaur. On my way to work one day, I saw a dinosaur created out of paper mache. It stood about ten feet high. I tried on several occasions to locate the owner, but never was successful. I was very much involved with running the campground and couldn't pursue the idea further.

A local citizen suggested I start a day camp for children that could run during the week. He said I could hire a couple of teachers who could run it. The children would enhance their education. He said, "You have a lot of things going for you," which was true. I investigated the idea thoroughly. "I'm not hiring a couple of school teachers to do something I'm not familiar with," I said. The idea was laid to rest.

Someone suggested I have a Fiddler's Contest. It got too complicated so we didn't have one.

We had a camper who was very much involved with nature. He used to write articles for a magazine. He wanted to take groups on Saturday or Sunday morning hikes on a hiking trail within the campground. Hikers would be taught about local trees, bushes, and rocks. It sounded like a good idea, and I said he should do it. The first group of about thirty people had a good time. The following Saturday he probably had about half as many, and the next Saturday he had less than that. He came back to me and said, "Well, I'm going to quit that job because all I have now are the kids without their parents. I'm becoming a babysitter and I don't like that." So that idea fizzled also.

35

Boys Will Be Boys

In the early years, there were several families that had young boys. We had to impose a curfew of ten thirty because most people didn't like a bunch of young boys roaming around the campground at night. We decided on a curfew because trying to get the boys to go to their campsites later at night was a challenge. Before the curfew, every time they hung out someplace I found them. In fact, I acquired the nickname of Elliott Ness because I was such a good sleuth, even though they played cat and mouse with me. Their pranks were not particularly destructive or even nasty. They were more like petty annoyances. Sometimes they stole a can of beer from a cooler that people left outside. They never did any harm to anybody, but we just didn't like them roaming around, especially at night.

The kids used to call me Elliott Ness from the TV show, "The Untouchables." I always seemed to be where things were happening. No one could ever figure out how I knew something was going to happen. But, we had Mrs. Dunphy, who ran the crafts program. She was quite the motivator, especially when the bigger kids came down and started yapping. Her ear was tuned quite well. She said to me, "Hey, "I'll be a lookout for you." I never said anything about it but, that way, I had a heads up on what was going on.

So, when the kids asked, "How'd you know what was going on?", I said, "I'm Elliott Ness. He knows everything."

Another time one of the parents asked me, "How about if we clean up the Quonset hut? It would be a good place for the kids to hang out and play. We'll take care of it."

"Sure," I said, "as long as you take care of it, fine." Everything went along pretty well. We had some campers on the other side of the hill. I always told everyone that if they saw something that didn't look right to please tell me, that it was for their safety as well as mine.

At different times, two women came to me and said, "Nelson,

something funny is going on up there at the hut."

"What's that?" I asked.

"Every once in awhile some kid comes down through and stops at the hut. He always has a big bag."

I couldn't very well tell the kids who said that because they would be labeled tattle-tales. So, I told the parents. They offered to hang out there with the kids for a while. After a time, the kid stopped coming through, and everything seemed okay. One night, though, it was quite dark and I decided to sneak up near the Quonset hut and hide in the bushes. I had a premonition that something might happen. I sat on the ground in the bushes to wait. The parents were there and the kids were playing. After awhile, the parents decided to leave. Immediately, one kid said, "I can't see them anymore. They're gone." Out came the beer. There were about ten kids. I let them gain a little momentum. Then I just casually walked over and stood on the side of the hut. It was dark but someone had a flashlight, so they caught me. "Oh," said one of the kids, "Nelson's here." They all laughed nervously.

I said, "This is the end of your fun. You guys can't control yourselves, so no more. Take off." Then I told the parents that I would close off the area. "You're doing right," I said, "but they're doing wrong, and I can't be an accessory to that kind of behavior."

Most of the boys were right with me if I was doing any kind of work like picking up stones or trying to get the place straightened out. Bobby Robinson even sat out in front of my camper waiting for me to come out so he could help me.

Bobby visited me years and years later, and gave me a big hug and squeeze. He said what he learned working for me — his ethics and his training — carried him through the rest of his life, and he came back to thank me for it. It's so rewarding for somebody to say something like that. It made me feel good. As a youngster, he and others had fun doing things at the campground.

Ricky Marin drove tractors at our campground. He later joined the army where he used his experience operating tractors. He wound up in Texas on a construction crew, and was quite happy about it. When he went out at night, he sometimes called me. He often told me how much he appreciated me letting him drive the tractor because not many young people who joined the army had driven tractors. The experience gave him a gateway to get into what he wanted to do. The only problem was that he called me in the evening. By my time it could be two in the morning because of the time difference. After a couple of times, I told him, "Hey, you've got to call me earlier," which he did. He was a great person.

I used to tell the boys all the time, "One boy is one boy, two boys is a half a boy. This means the more kids you have, the less things will get done. Three boys were no boys because when you get together, you start really clowning around." They always used to get a kick out of it. Even to this day two of them are still working for me. I often remind them that, "Two boys is only a half a boy." They agree and say they know the system.

At the end of the season I rounded up all the boys who helped me in the campground and took them up to Riverside Park in Massachusetts. When we went to the gate the first time, I paid for everybody, and they all went in and had a great time. The second time we went up, I said to the girl who sold tickets, "Isn't there a discount for this, my big family?"

She said, "Sure, go to the office, they'll take care of it."

So I went into the office remembering my grandmother saying years ago that everything is negotiable. The fellow there said right away, "We'll give you a twenty percent discount for all your kids." So it was worth opening my mouth. We had a great time there.

36

Drinking and Partying

When we first started the campground, drinking and partying were frequent. Drinking, especially, was a big problem. Everybody liked to drink. We didn't have any rules because we were just getting started. We expected people to go to bed at a reasonable time. So it wasn't too long after we got going that we realized we must develop rules about quiet hours. We set eleven in the evening as the time for quiet hours to begin. The problem was that some of the people would only begin to drink late at night.

I lived down the street. Every Sunday morning I came up and picked up the garbage to have it ready to go Monday morning. There were probably about forty or fifty campers at the very most, with approximately fifteen seasonal campers on site.

When I arrived one particular morning, it was reported to me by a camper that other campers on "A" Street were raising hell last night until two in the morning. The police came, a fistfight resulted, then an ambulance came. When I came down to pick up the garbage, I heard the story and started asking different campers about the incident. Most of them said there was a big party and they weren't there. I left at eight o'clock that night, so couldn't tell who was telling the truth. I figured it would be a long time before I found it out. It took me all day to collect the garbage, because each time I picked up the garbage, I talked to the people. Everybody had something to say. I didn't go home for lunch. When I asked, "What were you doing, Joe?" the answer was, "Oh, I wasn't there." I asked Mike, and he said, "Joe was right there all night. I saw him myself." By checkout time, at three o'clock, I had a picture in my mind of who was doing what. I went to each one who seemed to be a culprit and invited ten families to leave and not come back again. By this time, everyone was sober, and the stories were different. The women cried because they liked the campground. It was close to where they lived, and they came many times. I said, "You should have thought of it before you became drunk."

One camper had a baker's truck that was not registered. I told him to drive it up on the side of the hill where the horseshoe pits were. I gave him a week to get it out. Everybody else went and that was the end of that. It was quite a blow to lose that many seasonals in one shot.

The owner of the truck did not come back in the week I gave him. While the truck was parked, some children got into it and found some small recording disks. They threw them around. A camper came to me with one and said, "What are these disks?" I phoned the camper and said, "You better move this camper out of here because the kids got into it and they're going to destroy things." While the kids made a ruckus, campers in the immediate area saw what happened and heard what I was doing. One by one, before the day was out, they came up and shook hands with me and said, "We like what you're doing. They disturbed us, but as long as you're taking charge of it we have the feeling that you're trying to run a good place and we will be back."

Another incident was related to alcohol. One day a young boy told me there was a car in the campground up in G Area that was causing a lot of trouble. I checked but the car was gone.

Later that same evening the young boy came back to me and said, "Mr. Gustine, that car is up in G Area again." He continued to say that there were young boys in the truck who were harassing people. We called the police. They came and found out the boys were underage and were drinking. The police ordered them to get out of the campground.

In the early, early morning, I heard noises, so I grabbed my flashlight and set out to try to find out what was going on. I was alone, which was a mistake. In the dark, I went up back where the horseshoe pits are today. I couldn't find anybody, but I figured their car was some place. I turned around to head back home. I heard somebody running up in back of me. It was one of the culprits. I turned the flashlight on so I could look right in his face. He hit me in the face and knocked me down. I was taken to the hospital for a day. That's when I learned the lesson to never go out by myself.

Many things happened when people partied too much. One camper came in with his wife early in the season and told me that he was having problems in the marriage so he thought getting away camping would be good to help them get back together again. The only problem was that they chose a campsite where three or four couples did a lot of partying. The man's wife got involved with the partying, so after a couple of weeks, they went home. The husband said that they would be back shortly after they got their act together, so to speak. They did come back to the office. The wife said she wanted to go back to the same area they camped in before. I could see what was going to happen — more partying and more problems. When the wife left for a few minutes to go to the bathroom, I told the husband that I didn't think it was a good idea to go back to the same location. I said to him, "It would be easy for me to tell your wife that the sites are taken." Since he didn't want to create any trouble with his wife, he went along with her choice. Back they went to the partying area and began to party again. A few days later, the husband came up to where I was working. He wanted to shake hands with me and he said, "I should have taken your advice because my marriage has really fallen apart. There was too much partying, and we never had what you might call togetherness. So, we're leaving and it looks like my marriage is on the rocks. I want to thank you again for your advice. I was too foolish not to take it."

We had no rule regarding hard liquor in the Rec. hall in the beginning. One night a camper was imbibing in hard liquor. I didn't notice how much he was drinking. He became a pretty serious problem. I knew it was going to be a bigger problem, so I called the police to escort him out. Ever since then, we decided hard liquor would not be allowed in the Rec. hall. We could handle beer and wine because it takes a lot of it to get someone drunk. Since then, we haven't had any further problems with drinking in the Rec. hall.

Another issue we solved early on was a policy regarding campers who were friends. When two or more families came in together and were friends, I tried to find separate sites for them because I knew that eventually there would be trouble. It seemed that friends in close proximity to each other were likely to disagree and perhaps problems could worsen before their stay was over. Yet, if we placed families who were strangers to each other together, problems between them were rare. I was pretty successful with this policy.

37

Fires

Fires are always a possibility, no matter how hard we work to avoid them. The first involved a camper. He decided to take a job down by the shore and was commuting back and forth. The campground was halfway between his house in Hartford and the shore. When the camp closed, he asked me if he could stay for the rest of the fall. We found a spot where he could stay. We put in electricity for him. One day I was in Meriden where I lived, and my friend was listening to the police scanner. He heard there was a fire in Nelson's Campground. When he called to tell me, I became pretty nervous. I thought one of our buildings was burning. I called my neighbor near the camp. He told me that the fire department was already there and there was nothing left of the trailer. I realized it was the trailer that the fellow who worked down at the shore was living in. Thankfully, he was not there. I decided to drive to the camp anyway. When I got there, all I saw was his iron. Everything else was gone.

The second fire was in E Area. A young couple just purchased a small, used trailer. The price paid was way below market value because somebody just wanted to get rid of it. Instead of insuring it for what it was actually worth, the husband insured it for what he paid for it. That was a big mistake. After they left one morning, the toaster in their trailer caught fire and burned it down. By the time people saw the fire and called the fire department, there was nothing left. The owner collected from his insurance company. That's when he realized he didn't insure it for enough. The amount of money he got was not enough money to buy another camper. They said goodbye. Their days of camping were over.

A young boy in the camp was playing with matches in a big field where the hay was about a foot high. It is where Glenn's and Bruce's houses are today. The child lit a match, which the wind caught and soon the field was ablaze. A neighbor saw the fire from across the street and called the fire department. By the time the fire department arrived, the fire was already at the camp entrance. I was at my own cottage nursing trouble with my shoulders when somebody called me and said there was a fire at the campground. When I hear "fire," I immediately think a building is on fire. I became pretty nervous when I heard the fire trucks going by. Then I found out what it was, a big grass fire, so it didn't do too much damage. The next day, the father of the little boy found out his son set the fire. He and his son came up to me, and the boy, who was obviously frightened and nearly petrified, apologized for starting the fire. The father said to me, "I want you to give him a good lashing because he needs it. I can't have him setting fires." Of course, I didn't touch the boy, but I thought it was really nice of the father to make him apologize. He insisted on paying for the damage, but we lost only grass and some small evergreen trees. I said, "You were man enough to come over and tell me about it, we'll just shake hands and forget about it."

38

Fooling the Children

I needed another small pickup truck. I bought a used pickup that was also a dump truck. The idea of its dual uses amazed me. I loved it. One day there was a large group of campers in the field. They needed wood for campfires. We always let campers who helped us chop down trees pick any wood they wanted. I went to the group when I saw them congregating and said, "I have a truck into which you can throw the wood. I have an idea. So wait a moment." Then I went to a group of children who were hanging around and said, "Come with me and load the truck. You can pick up the wood and put it in the truck. Your fathers will then take it out of the truck where we'll build a campfire." They liked the idea. They always wanted to help anyway.

I drove them up the road into the woods, and they filled the truck up with firewood. Since there was no longer any room for them in the truck, they ran alongside the truck back to the area where everyone congregated. One of the children said to his father, "Okay, Dad, we loaded it, and now you have to unload it."

I said to one of the fathers, "Come over here a minute." Then I said, "See that lever right there? Pull that lever." So he pulled that lever, and to his surprise the noise was so loud that everybody ran. The dump truck dumped all the wood in a big pile. I can still hear the children now because they were really upset.

Once we had a pig roast. At the time I had two pigs where I have my goats today. The pigs were like pets. People loved to just watch them. Two boys and a woman were standing at the cage looking at the pigs. I walked up to them about the same time. One of the young boys said, "Oh, there's the pig for the pig roast." The woman started to go crazy. She was yelling and screaming, and she went into a screaming fit. I tried to tell her that those were my pets, but she wouldn't listen. She kept going and going until it became serious. I tried to placate her, but she wouldn't calm down. Finally, she walked away.

39

Expanding the Campground

Glenn, Michele, Nelson, Bruce, and Mildred Gustine
Image used with permission from National Association of RV Parks and Campgrounds (ARVC)

As time went on, we needed more help. Mil and I couldn't handle everything ourselves. We taught our sons about working on the grounds when they were old enough to work. They both went to school close by and worked every evening and weekend.

Later on, Glenn went to work for a restaurant chain. He advanced to manager quite rapidly. While working at one of the stores he met Michele. A short time later in early spring, he invited Michele to come to the campground for the weekend. She later joined Mildred in running the store and office. We were very pleased when the relationship grew. Although Michele was a city girl, she quickly learned how to do without running water in the bathroom in the trailer during the off season. We had to carry water in from the well. Michele stuck with it, but I don't think she ever adjusted to the outhouse. Several years later, Glenn and Michele were married. In their free time, they both helped run the campground. One day Glenn came home and said to

Mil and me, "Michele and I would like to quit our jobs at the restaurant and come run the campground full time." For Mil and me it was a dream come true. I told him that they were certainly welcome, but we would have to increase the number of campsites if we were going to support another family. At the time, we had over one hundred sites. Glenn and I went to the town zoning board and applied to build a total of up to four hundred ten campsites. It was approved. Both sons worked hard to ready the new campsites, and are well on their way toward the approved number.

Campsites

Aerial view of the campground

Gustine's RV Sales

F Area full house

40

The Tent

Vendor sale under the tent

On several occasions we had two or more groups that wanted to use the Rec. hall. But, it was just not big enough to accommodate more than one group. A camper said to me, "You know, I saw an ad in the paper from a tent company. They have a large tent for sale. It's a used tent."

I said, "That's what we need when the Rec. hall can't accommodate everyone." I called the company and learned it was two cities away from us. The size was 40 x 60 feet, which was what we needed. So, we bought it. It lasted for quite a few years. As time went on, it began to deteriorate. When the wind blew, it was hard to keep it tied down. We had to make sure we were out there to hold it down, so we didn't lose it or precipitate an accident. On one occasion it developed a large rip. It was obviously worn out. After several more years, I decided to get rid of the tent. Then we built a permanent pavilion in the same spot. It is still there today. It's also 40 x 60 feet and serves quite a few functions during the season.

41

Snacks and Other Meals

Several campers were business minded or owned businesses. One was Mr. Pizza. Every Saturday he took orders for pizzas and gave them to his son who owned a pizza shop in the next town. The son delivered them around seven thirty in the evening. Everyone who purchased a pizza came to the field to pick up their pizzas. This made for a lot of camaraderie among the campers, and many friendships developed as a result. Mr. Pizza did this for several years. The business increased to about fifty to seventy-five pizzas on a Saturday night. By the time he stopped selling pizzas, he told me the most he sold was ninety-five pizza orders in one day. That was quite a record.

After we built the Rec. hall addition, we had room for a snack bar. We were discussing how to go about it when a couple came in. The husband said, "I have a closed-in truck that I used for a snack bar on the side of the road. I'm not using it now. I'll bring it in if you want, and we'll run it." I liked the idea so we agreed to do it.

But there was one problem. They had a peculiar way of getting the orders prepared. The wife took the order, passed it to her husband who cooked the hamburgers or other menu items. She wouldn't take another order until the first one was cooked. The customer line grew longer and longer, and people were upset about having to wait so long. One man in line with his wife and kids got tired of waiting, so he jumped in the car and drove down the street to a fast food restaurant. He bought a hamburger and French fries. He came back with them and sat down in his chair in the line eating it while his wife and kids were still waiting to place their order. Now, the whole line got cranky and upset, and some choice words were thrown around.

After a month, I fired the snack bar team. About a year later, I realized we still needed a snack bar. Campers told me they wanted one, but that it should be run efficiently. I purchased the necessary equipment and hired the workers who gave better service. Today we have a successful snack bar. I always learned from my mistakes!

A group of men asked me if they could sell fruit and vegetables in the camp. They said they would do it by driving a station wagon to Hartford to pick up the fresh food. I said, "That's great, but there are two rules you must follow. No one rides on the tailgate, and no one drinks beer. I don't want anyone to get hurt." Their business was very successful. Campers liked the service. They even asked the guys to be sure to bring back certain fruits and vegetables they particularly liked.

Like every good idea someone has to spoil it. One Saturday they came back from the farmers' market later than usual. The first thing I saw as I drove by was the station wagon speeding towards the campsite a little distance away. Some men were on the tailgate. One had a can of beer in his pocket, and the other had a can of beer in his hand. I felt I had to put a stop to this business. Quite a few people complained because they really enjoyed the fresh vegetables and fruits that were delivered almost to their doors. The men who broke my rules spoiled a good thing. I was afraid that someone drinking beer was going to fall off the tailgate and get hurt. Then it would be my fault so my insurance rates would surely increase.

42

The Accident

Two campers from California camped in our D Area, a woman and her husband. One day the husband came to the office and told Mil that he needed a doctor. He said, "My wife did a stupid thing. She fell off our trailer step." We usually didn't make a habit of recommending doctors, but this time Mildred felt sorry for the woman. She gave the husband several doctors' names in the area. We found out later she broke her ankle so badly that they decided to return to California.

Six months went by. I practically forgot the incident. Then I received a notice that we were being sued by the couple because of the fall on their campsite, although she fell off her own trailer step. I took the notice to my insurance company and a pre-trial hearing was set up, which I attended. At the pre-trial hearing, I found out the couple sent an engineer to measure the ground for depressions using a six-foot ruler, or leveler. She said that she tripped in the campsite because of the depressions in the ground. She didn't notice them as she walked. They also produced several photos of the campsite clearly showing they were on site number 6. The lawyer spent about thirty minutes discussing campsite number 6. He also insisted on seeing my maintenance records. I told him I was a one-man operation, and I didn't have any records. When it was my turn to talk at the hearing, as many times as I could, I repeated what the husband said about his wife falling off her own trailer step. I waited till the very end and I said, "I do not understand why you are spending so much time talking about site number 6." In my hand I had the registration form signed by her husband that had registered them to site number 8. Then I repeated what the husband said about his wife doing a stupid thing, and that they had camped on site number 8. It was a technicality, but worth emphasizing. After that, the hearing came to a close. I never heard any more regarding the law suit. Whether they settled or not I never knew, never heard.

43

Gate Crasher

It was a bright Sunday afternoon, and my wife and I sat on our porch relaxing as we watched the world go by. Other campers were preparing for a planned powwow. A camper who was going to participate in the powwow came flying up the road, plowing right through the gate. The gate was in shambles, and pieces of it

The gate into the campground

went flying all over the place, but the driver just kept going. Later on that afternoon he came into the office, telling Michele that the gate came down on him, smashed his windshield, and cracked it in several places. He asked her for a form to fill out a complaint for our insurance company. Michele didn't know what happened, so she gave him the form. I think you have to do that. Then I spoke to him. I said, "I sat on the porch with my wife and watched you drive right through. You didn't even stop! You just broke right through there."

He insisted, "No, I didn't."

Then his wife came up to me and said, "He's got a pass. I don't know why he would do that."

"I don't know why he would do it either, but all I know is what I saw," I said. We spoke back and forth for a day and a half. Finally, I knew this had to be resolved, so I said to him, "Well, I'll send the form to the insurance company but I'm gonna put a note on the bottom that says I watched you drive right through my gate, and we probably will charge you for the gate. We're going to have the gate checked to see what happened to it. I know that the gate itself broke, and the mechanism could have broken, too, so I don't know how much that will cost."

My statement seemed to make him a little nervous. He must have realized he was wrong. We forwarded the form to the insurance company with my note which said, "Don't pay this guy because he drove right though my gate and broke it." The insurance company called me and we discussed the incident. He and his wife left that day and I've never seen him since. I guess it was fortunate that we were there when he came through so we witnessed exactly what happened.

44

No Smoking

All my life I've been an anti-smoker. I never cared for anything about smoking. Saturdays were laundry days for me. One time I was in the laundromat reading while waiting for my clothes to get done. A mother was there with her young daughter also waiting for their laundry to get done. I didn't know her, and she didn't know me. She was smoking. As she got ready to leave I said, "It's really too bad that when your daughter grows up and has her own family, the chances are you'll probably miss it because you've been smoking all the time." She gave me a dirty look, grabbed her daughter by the hand, picked up the laundry with the other hand, and out the door she went.

It's hard to believe about a year later when I was in the camp laundromat, a woman came in who now thought she knew who I was. She said, "Aren't you Nelson from the campground?"

"Yes," I said.

"Do you remember me?"

"No," I answered.

"Well, last year, I was in here with my daughter. You were telling me the chances were that because I was a smoker, I wouldn't be around when she got married and had her family, and I'd miss out on that. I left in a huff."

"I remember," I said as I smiled at her. No point in having enemies, I thought.

"When I got home that night, I looked in the mirror, and everything you said started ringing bells in my head. I got pretty upset that you said that, but I got even more upset because I realized you were right." She continued to tell me that because she loves her daughter so much, she didn't want to miss that part of her life. "So I decided to go cold turkey with cigarettes," she continued. "I threw all my cigarettes away, and I haven't smoked since."

"You gotta be kidding me," I said.

"No, and you are responsible. So, when I came here today to your camp, I decided I was going to tell you." It turned out that she came once in a while during the summer, for about two years, but I had no contact with her. I guess by this time the business grew to the point where sometimes I didn't meet new campers. She continued, "I'm so happy you said that because I haven't smoked since last year. I still have my little girl, and I'm looking forward to when she gets married, like you said. I hope to be here for her because I quit smoking."

I went over and put a mark on the wall and said, "Touché. I've said that to quite a few people, but you're the first one who ever responded in a positive way. I thank you and appreciate that you came back and told me that."

Some time later, I was involved in another group where I was after a fellow all the time about smoking. He said to me, "You know, Nelson, you have a store in the campground."

"That's right."

"So you sell cigarettes there?"

I said, "Yes, we do."

"Isn't that kind of hypocritical? You're selling cigarettes and telling people not to smoke?"

I said, "I guess you're gonna win this argument." We used to argue almost all the time about that. "You hit a real soft spot there, and I'm telling you that when I go back home, that's the end of the cigarettes at my campground." That was five or six years ago, and we haven't sold a cigarette since.

45

Awards

Al Brilliant implemented a lot of ideas. He became what I used to call "the self-appointed mayor of G Area." Every time we had a seasonal potluck supper, he gave me an award. All the awards were created by Al, and each one had a meaning. One award was his favorite. It was for the last outhouse on the property. Another one was for the time we put electric meters in the campground. When we raised the fee for electricity, he gave me a mounted electric meter. On our twenty-fifth anniversary, he commemorated it with an award also.

Al Brilliant at potluck dinner

45th Anniversary Award

One year we decided instead of having a potluck supper, we'd have the supper catered. Everybody liked the idea. We had the catered dinner, but it didn't turn out as successfully as we expected because we ran out of food. The following year, as an award, he gave me one knife, which is not very commendable for a restaurant. We now have over twenty awards. The originals are mounted on the wall in the Rec. hall today, and if you visit, you can take a look at them.

Awards given out at potluck dinners by Al Brilliant

46

Revisiting the Campground

Quite a few times over the years grown men have come back to the campground to visit. Often, they have asked me if I remembered them. Sometimes, I didn't, so I said, "No, I don't remember you."

Their responses would be along the lines of, "Well, I camped here in my teens with my sister and family and we had such a great time."

Then I said, "Let me ask you a question. Did I ever bring you back to your father and mother holding you by the back of the neck because you did something naughty?"

If they said, "No," I said, "Well, if that's the case I wouldn't remember you." I was always gratified when people told me that when they were in the campground camping, they had so much fun in their early years they thought about it all their life. Most enjoyable was when they got married, had a family, and came back so their children could have the same experiences as they did. It made me feel good.

One family that camped with me had a young son, an early teenager. He was trouble from day one. If there was trouble, he was in the middle of it. When this family left, the father told me he could not camp with his son because he was too much trouble. He felt he had to stay home where he could watch him all the time. Although the parents really loved camping, the boy spoiled it for them, and they decided to sell their camper. Years and years later, I thought I recognized the father coming in as a visitor. And sure enough it was him. He told me that his son, the little brat, had married and had a family of his own. The father wanted to come back into Nelson's to relive some of his experiences. He said, "What am I doing? I don't have a camper because my son made me sell it, but now I'm here to visit him. I can't even believe it myself." He also said that once he sold the camper, he never had enough money to buy one again, so they had to give up camping. He continued, "But now my son's camping, and I'm visiting him because it's so much fun. I can't believe it."

47
Campers' Favorite Memories

Al Brilliant was a long-time camper. He had a knack for asking questions and needling Nelson. He always gave Nelson a hard time. For example, at the beginning of the week, Al picked up a flier listing activities for the week. When Al came down to the Rec. hall and picked one up, Nelson said to him, "Why are you picking up that flier? You don't come down to these activities. You don't do anything."

"Well," Al said, "I just wanted to know what you have scheduled."

Other times, Al appeared at the Rec. hall. Nelson said, "Oh, you came down off the mountain." These kinds of comments probably made people think Al was like Moses.

Goings On In Area G
Contributed by Al Brilliant

In Area G there was a kind of eccentric group of campers; that is, they were very opinionated. One never knew what to expect. However, they always got together socially such as at a picnic. But, they couldn't always decide what to have at the picnic or what to do. Whatever management wanted, they would be against. I guess it was just their nature. After all, campers complained about one thing or another. To help alleviate the tensions, a Board of Directors was appointed. It was also decided that if folks wanted to go to Area G, they would have to apply for membership and be approved by the Board of Directors.

When the Board had a meeting, a banner was raised that said,

"Area G Board of Directors Meeting." Every person there was like a sub-committee that supported whatever he or she wanted to do. For example, Jack was in charge of public works. We told him we wanted a sidewalk here or street lighting there, and he went to bat for it at the meeting. There was always a list of demands for management to implement. Among themselves they moaned or groaned, but the best part was that the meetings brought us all together. I became the self-appointed mayor once they decided they needed a leader.

When we first started camping, we were down in the field in the tenting area. Then we progressed up — that is, those of us who came regularly. We always booked in advance of all long weekends and holidays. Then one guy said to me, "Well, you know, you did this and that. Do the math." So, the whole group of us went seasonal in 1982 because it was cheaper. When I told people I was going camping, they said, "Well, you're camping? It must be rough."

You want to know how we camp? They probably figured we had a Coleman tent, or something like that. I explained it was a tent more like a chateau. Then they wanted to know what we had in our campers. I said we had a microwave, an air conditioner, a heater, refrigerator, and a queen-sized bed. The reaction was often a question. "You call that camping?" I told them we did.

These people were impressed and eventually some of them joined us. Eventually, we all wound up in Area G. We liked Nelson's because it was wooded and the management was good. The only person running it during the week was Mildred, and we liked her. Nelson would come down on weekends, I think, to make a big appearance. Like he said, "I'm the manager." Meanwhile, it seemed to me that Mildred was doing all the work.

We had an American flag as well as one called the "Area G flag." Occasionally we had a parade. Jack and Elaine were the color guards who marched at the front bearing the Area G flag. During one ceremony music played, and I was the emcee. I introduced everyone including Joan, Mary, Joe, Kent and myself. The first two were the sergeant-at-arms and the speaker of the house. They escorted the Gustine family up to the podium. As Nelson walked up, the band played "Hail to the Chief." You should have seen the expression on

Nelson's face. He made us think he was the President with that broad smile and stature.

Like clockwork, a jet flew right over the parade, as if it was meant to do so. Another time we wanted to unveil a plaque. We put a black bunting with a drawstring over it, and designated Mildred to draw the string. She seemed nervous because she thought when she pulled the string, a door would open and a skeleton would come out and get her. Nelson, do you remember that?

"Yes," Nelson replied. "I could see she was so scared, she was afraid to pull the drawstring. So, I did it."

The music continued to play, and we prepared for our picnic. The plaque was for the dedication of Area G as an historical landmark. It looked like a plaque you'd put on a famous building. Well, this area was famous. We had a lot of fun there.

Precious Memories

by Cora (Pierce) Sciarra

It may be hard for anyone to believe how much of a difference the Gustines made in my life. They certainly did this for me, and many others at a special place, Nelson's Family Campground.

Mildred Gustine saw my needs and took me "under her wing." She allowed me to help her at the store and the cottages. She taught me SO many things I used in my adult life. She taught me things I never knew. The time we spent together was precious! We went to tag sales which taught me to be efficient with money. I watched her juggle the campground business and a home life which taught me how to run a business and household at the same time. She also taught me about the importance of communication in relationships. These are just a few examples of what a city girl who went to a campground learned from loving, caring owners!

Nelson Gustine taught me plenty directly and indirectly. I was fortunate to learn a lot by observing his gift of how he handled people. These skills came in handy in my adult life, as I tried to follow his example of a calm, respectful demeanor, no matter how difficult a person was. He was a quiet man, who always taught something wise when he spoke. He kindly shared many words of wisdom throughout my seven years I worked with him. Any time an opportunity to share wisdom and knowledge with me was there, he explained these important things about life to me. This is another example I still try to follow with others today, to pass along to the next generation.

As the years went on, they gave me more responsibilities. It is impossible to describe what this did for me. I felt like Nelson and Mildred were my second parents. They were so unconditionally loving. They reached out to me in so many ways far beyond what ANY employer would ever do. We had so many "talks" that, to this day, I remember and use. I even try to follow their Godly example in how they reached out to others with people who work for our family now. It is a tribute to them, I hope!

I doubt anyone would EVER think an experience at a campground could be so life altering. It continues today. Although I am not at the campground now, I feel a closeness to the campground, several past campers, and especially the Gustine family, that lacks words. I will forever be grateful for the blessings that came through Nelson's Family Campground.

Tween Times

Contributed by Cindy (St. Martin) Herbert

We teens went up on the dam of the pond and sat on the hill to talk at night. We laid down and looked at the stars and the constellations.

Once in a while – more often than not – at the end of the night, we stripped off our clothes and dove off the dock where the paddle boats were anchored to skinny dip. Sometimes it was not so nice because there was algae. We never knew what was in the water. It did not feel too good. We used to go out to a "sandbar" to the right of the raft in the middle of the pond, but stopped after what we think was a beaver popped his head out of the pond. That scared us. Nelson Gustine never caught us, but the beaver did!

There was a curfew that was made for the teenagers because the teenagers were noisy and disturbed others. Since no one "came clean" to tell Nelson or Mildred Gustine who it was who made the noise, the curfew was instituted. I think the time was ten o'clock, but we never followed it. We were mad because we felt it was unfair. We used to go up to the Quonset hut by Area E. We hid out so we were not caught since we were doing "naughty things." One night Nelson Gustine came to the Quonset hut in the station wagon. All we saw were headlights coming, so we all ran in different directions to our sites. We did not want to be caught. I ran through the field with a couple of others from nearby sites. As we crossed the road approaching our site, we finally were able to evade Mr. Gustine. I still remember and feel the pit in my stomach since I knew I was in big trouble if I was caught.

Under what was then the store was a pay phone where people got "zapped" a lot. There once was an electrical storm going on and the pay phone rang. Although I was wet and in bare feet, I ran to answer it. I was REALLY zapped!

One time, a group of teens lifted Dolores Dunphy's Volkswagen Beetle up and carried it under the pavilion. She was VERY surprised when she came out of work. She laughed, but wondered HOW she would get it out. Her boys were involved with it as well. It was a funny sight to see!

I remember, also, when the young camper who had epilepsy had a seizure while he tried to swim to the raft and drowned. It was very sad for all of us.

I have to mention my precious trolls that are either sitting at the bottom of the pond or are totally deteriorated. As we sat on the dock at night, I placed them into the pond to show my friend they could float. After a period of time they quickly filled with water and sank fast – too fast to save them.

Another neat event that happened was Saturday night pizza delivery. All families had to do was order and pay ahead, and the car showed up and beeped the horn a series of times to alert us they were there. We got to "eat out" without leaving the campground. There was no snackbar at the camp then, but the Gustines went out of their way to make it possible for families to stay by the campfire to enjoy time together.

It was really nice to have the small open area behind us, that was usually not very full, and pick blackberries and blueberries. There was plenty to pick which kept me busy and out of trouble for a while.

Another precious place to me near our site (Area "A") was a huge boulder by the bathroom where a nearby camper, Ricky, and I met late at night. We sat and talked from the top of it. I have good memories from there, since we talked about EVERYTHING!

Although I do not keep in touch with most of my past friends from the campground, one of the campers then, Darlene, is now married to my neighbor's brother. I sometimes see her when she and her husband, Bobby, stop in at my work to eat. We talk about memories from the campground, which always bring smiles.

Midnight Visitor

It was the summer of 1978 and, for a little girl from the inner city of Newark, New Jersey, these weekends were the highlight of the year, especially this particular weekend. My parent's friends and their small daughter would be joining us. They never camped before.

Our very first night that weekend became one that most of our family and most of the "D Streeters" never forgot! Sometime after midnight, my mom woke to something pushing her side of the air mattress up from underneath the tent. "Jimmy, Jimmy! There's something under the tent!" My father, who for safety reasons always slept with a machete under his side of the bed, hoisted the machete. With a "Thump" he brought the flat side down on the wiggling lump under the tent.

Just as the rest of the tent's occupants woke to the unholy screech emitted by the unknown intruder, the most pungent, indescribable smell wafted through the air. It seemed to permeate everything – air, pores, clothes, sleeping bags, and even the tent itself! As you may have guessed, our visitor was a skunk.

I could share many more memories – a first crush, a first heart-break, my first dance, and many others. All of these are from Nelson's, and all define the woman I grew to be. All are reasons I felt compelled to bring my son here, to this wonderful place where children can for-get the dangers of society. They can make friends that will return year after year and, hopefully, thirty years from now share one or two of their favorite memories with their children or future campers.

"Wild Bill's" Caricatures

Bill Taylor, also known as "Wild Bill" is a former school teacher who began doing caricatures in the 1980s. Here is his story below:

I was at the RV show in the old New Haven Coliseum, which was the hub of many events in New Haven. While I did caricatures, a very good looking, middle-aged woman stood over my left shoulder. She stood there looking at what I did, not saying anything. I went to ask her what she wanted.

Thank goodness I said nothing. After a few more subjects, she said, "Give me one of those flyers." I did, and the rest was history. You see, the woman was Mildred Gustine who, with her husband, ran Nelson's Family Campground in East Hampton, Connecticut.

They had me there once, twice, three, and finally four times in the camp season to do caricatures.

When I did this a couple of years my wife, Charlotte, came with me as my color artist. I introduced myself as "Wild Bill," and turned to my wife and said, "This is 'Sweet Charli.'" This always got, if not a chuckle, a smile.

I did the caricatures and told stories or gags one told in mixed company. One thing I said that got the children off guard was, "What is your favorite subject in school?" With a slight pause, I added, "Besides boys," if it was a girl, or "Besides girls," if it was a boy. This caused a smile from ear to ear!

Treated as Family

I began to camp at Nelson's in my early twenties in the field. After years of camping in the field, my family decided to buy a trailer and become seasonal campers.

We loved going to the dances on Saturday nights. We enjoyed hanging with our friends around a campfire until the wee hours of the morning. Playing horseshoes on Saturdays and Sundays also became a tradition.

We were always treated as family at Nelson's, and not just another customer. I will forever be grateful for that.

The Brook, The Rock, The Boy

The year was 1971, the first year our family of three camped here. The campsite was close to the brook that enters the pond.

This boy of ten years had no fishing pole, but had an idea he would try. He found a rock big enough to lie on and waited patiently. In time, it paid off, as he grabbed hold of a small trout! He ran, laughing, back up to his campsite to show his dad. Today, this boy is a skilled fisherman, but now with a fishing pole!

Reliving My Childhood

Keri Entwistle

I just want to thank Nelson and everyone else involved for allowing me to relive my childhood at your campground March 12, 2010. We had a BLAST! I remembered where everything was after twenty two years so well, it was like I had never left.

My favorite memories were at my grandparent's camp spot, which I remembered because of the special rock that was where we used to leave food for the birds and squirrels.

There was the big creek that we used to cross with our grandpa to see the "rock quarry," as we called it. The "little lake" (pond) with the raft that I have a beautiful picture of with my grandmother and me walking along the beach is still there. So many things throughout the park remained the same for all of these years.

My parents LOVED time spent here with their family. We all have some of the best memories of our lives at your special campground. I guess you had no idea that you touched so many lives in such a special way. No words can express the joy you brought to me. I will never forget you.

Then there was the camp store where my grandma bought me all of those forest green Nelson's sweatshirts. I also loved to visit Mildred Gustine in the store. One time she was organizing some kind of scavenger hunt with "fool's gold." My cousin and I did not know, and started finding them around the Rec. hall and pool area. We thought we were rich. We made the mistake of showing them to Mildred, and she made us re-hide them. We were so upset. All of the other kids ended up finding them before we got back up there, so we went crying to grandpa back at the campsite. He took us to town to buy gold spray paint to make our own.

You are wonderful people, and I thank you for everything you did for me. I will treasure the memories, old and new, forever and ever.

I saw the "Help Wanted" sign there and I wanted to stay. I told my friend to go back home. I did not want to leave. It is crazy how one special place in your life can be so powerful. I do not know what else to say except, "Nelson and Mildred, the 'New Crew', and beautiful campground will never be forgotten."

The Volkswagen Beetle Gang

It started as a campfire story about how one of our "gang" put a Volkswagen Beetle on someone's front porch. The camp's Volkswagen Beetle owner was certain it could not be done, so it became a challenge to us to prove it could. We moved his Beetle to the "spillway", the opposite side of the pond when there were no campsites there, behind the Area B bathroom, and the grapevines, which are now Area F. In order to stop having to hunt for the Volkswagen every morning, the owner decided to chain the car to a large tree on his site. We simply made the chain shorter each night, so that he eventually had to find a smaller tree.

Now came our opportunity to dig a hole in the field where construction was in progress, cut down the tree the Beetle was chained to, and move both to the field. Since the rule of the campground was absolutely no cutting of trees, we knew we were in danger of being kicked out of the campground, so we waited in the bushes for the owner the next morning.

After a good laugh and some shouting, the owner took the Beetle and chain to work. The rest of us filled in the hole with rocks, which were always plentiful. We then cut up the pine tree for that night's fire.

Until now, many never realized this was a true story, but many of us are fortunately still camping here some thirty years later. Thanks for the fond memories! The Volkswagen Beetle Gang

Fishing

When I was fourteen years old, I was a seasonal camper at Nelson's. My dad bought a small row boat and paid a guy on Lake Pocotopaug to tie it up to his dock. My friends and I walked down to the lake carrying the oars and fishing poles. We fished all day, and rowed around the lake. Some of my best memories are from Nelson's when I was a kid.

48

Reminiscing

Nelson Gustine at the campground entrance

At the beginning of Memorial Day weekend in 2009, one of the largest weekends of the summer besides Fourth of July and Labor Day, I rode through the campground. It was forty-five years after we built it.

It was interesting for me. The place was mobbed with people, children, and dogs all running around having a good time. It sure was a good feeling to think of all that my wife and I created for people to come and enjoy. Unfortunately, on April 15th, 2009, we lost Mildred.

As I traveled to the different parts of the campground, I couldn't help but reminisce a little. As beginning campers we were always happy to be at the campground, find a nice camp spot, and a place to relax. I remembered building everything, grading all the land like it was yesterday.

One of the first things we needed was water closer to the campsite and then we had to have electricity, which was a great improvement. We also installed flush toilets and showers. Then we were ready for the big time.

Entertainment was important, so we began to show movies at

the pavilion. It was followed by dances and bingo, more movies, disc jockeys, magicians, hypnotists, potluck suppers, and so forth. Camp was no longer simply sitting around a campfire. People called to see what activities we were having at the time they wanted to come. We put up activity sheets in the pavilion and on the bathrooms that listed the events going on.

When we first built the Rec. hall we needed something more to create interest in it beside dances. We provided pin ball machines, a pool table, a ping-pong table, and video games.

Activities in the Rec. hall

The pool and Rec. hall

The playground

The pavilion behind the Rec. hall

The pond

Old Home Day float - 2005

Today we have six bathroom buildings. We have a laundry building that was previously our small pavilion and store that we first built. We have a large 50 x 100-foot recreation hall, a store, a snack bar, a miniature golf course, volleyball, and basketball. We have a good-sized playground, a large pool, and a soccer field. We also have a large open pavilion that we use for parties and activities. We have dances, potluck dinners, bingo, a diamond scavenger hunt, and a men's cross-dressing contest.

We have the two-acre pond for swimming and fishing. Children

Bathroom B

Bathroom C

Pavilion laundry and showers

Bathroom G

Bathroom I

Bathroom T

are always down there hoping to catch the biggest fish. When someone does catch a large fish, we record it and post it on the wall in the recreation hall. We reward the family whose member catches the largest fish each month with a free weekend. This creates a bit of commotion and competition. We don't take their word for it. The catcher has to bring the fish to the girl behind the counter who measures it and records the statistics. Since the fish is alive, it is jumpy, and the girl gets excited, but it's a good thing.

I can't believe how we grew. We started the campground with forty sites. After the first two years we had one hundred sites. We had telephone service at the campground. Then the big thing was TV at all sites. Computer hookups came and were popular throughout the camp. Cell phones were next. Sometimes it was a challenge to get people to come to the events because they were too busy and absorbed in their cell phones. However, the good thing about cell phones is we no longer need telephone service at the campground. Today, we have about three hundred fifty campsites. Each site has electricity, cable TV, and water. There is also a group camping field.

I used to be in the office, making contact with everyone coming and going. I can't always do that now. Whereas I used to meet people one-on-one, today when I drive through the campground, I know maybe only ten families in the whole place. Some have been here thirty years. Every year, we lose some camping families for one reason or another. Many of my old friendships with the old-timers are dwindling down with everything else in life.

It is now 2012. I once again think back to when my wife and I first set up the campground and how things have changed. Now, my sons, Glenn and Bruce, and daughter-in-law, Michele, run the campground. Having our two boys and one daughter-in-law interested in running, and actually operating the campground could not have made Mildred and me happier. They have assumed all the responsibilities that go with it. I'm more of an on-looker and consultant, although I still know everything that goes on! I appreciate how they have taken over. They do a great job.

They acquired another campground called Wolf's Den in East Haddam, Connecticut. Also, we initiated a full-fledged RV sales and service department which is located in Nelson's Campground. I am so proud of all our great accomplishments.

It's difficult to remember everything that happened during the last forty-eight years, but I tried to remember as much as I could. As I remembered it, I recorded it. So things are not exactly the way they happened. It's just the way I remembered them.

As I reflect on all the wonderful people I met, who helped my dreams come true with my campground and family, I would like to thank them all for their love, support, and help.

But the big question in my mind has always been, "What is next?"

Bye, Bye